From Problem-Solving to Responsible Decision-Making

From Problem-Solving to Responsible Decision-Making

by

Norma S. Guerra and Abelardo Villarreal
University of Texas at San Antonio

emerald
PUBLISHING

United Kingdom – North America – Japan –
India – Malaysia – China

Emerald Publishing Limited
Emerald Publishing, Floor 5, Northspring, 21-23 Wellington Street, Leeds LS1
4DL

First edition 2025

British Library Cataloguing in Publication Data
A catalogue record for this book is available from the British Library

ISBN: 978-1-83708-507-1 (Print paperback)
ISBN: 978-1-83708-506-4 (Print hardback)
ISBN: 978-1-83708-508-8 (Ebook)
ISBN: 978-1-83708-509-5 (EPUB)

CONTENTS

SECTION II: RESPONSIBLE DECISION-MAKING

PREFACE

From Problem-Solving to Responsible Decision-Making relates the story of problem-solving with life examples from the Castillo and Mendoza families who emigrated to the U.S. and how they explored human development challenges, conflict management, and change as critical elements of self, self-identity, and community. The inspiration for this project began with a strong bond between a mother, Rosie Mendoza Guerra, who has a passion for collecting names, pictures, and stories, and her daughter, Norma Guerra, the book's lead author, whose imagination and wisdom led to the creation of this book. Each time we (aunts, uncles, and cousins Evelyn Bollinger, and Deborah Shandley) met for family chats, conversations circled back to our glorious and shared past. As photo albums appeared, new questions surfaced about what, who, and why the family took the path they did. What were the challenges, how were they met? And then there were discussions involving the problem-solving activities and consequences. The thirst for more knowledge led to months and years of research (i.e., deeds, licenses, and documented transactions).

One day, at an informal family gathering, a shift in our usual conversations culminated in the inclusion of another cousin, Dr. Rebecca Karimi, an archaist, who had conducted intensive research on the Mendoza family. She had a collection of oral histories from many of the Mendoza grandchildren, now elders or deceased. She graciously shared those Mendoza-recorded narratives. The information gathered from these narratives provided the foundation for Chapters 1 and 6. Thanks to Rebecca, Evelyn, and Deborah for their open willingness to share collected data, stories, and research. We faced a challenge in describing momentous life events in a

From Problem-Solving to Responsible Decision-Making,
pp. ix–x
www.emeraldgrouppublishing.com

non-glamorized manner, but we managed to be objective in our descriptions of events shared in this book. Still with the collaboration of Dr. Abelardo Villarreal, a researcher, educator, and writer, along with my family, this book's content fulfilled the goal of highlighting the nuances of the family's decision-making events and their impact on later generations.

We also managed to focus on those events that displayed the family's commitment to honesty and fairness, as shown through their desire to adapt to this country. These events exemplify problems they faced and describe the prevailing problem-solving approaches: straightforward and complex; the latter requiring a collaborative effort to implement responsible decision-making skills. Four critical features of these problem-solving approaches included: (1) context—environment and setting; (2) actors—persons affected by decisions; (3) problem complexity—including problems with multiple challenges broken down into smaller problem-solving events; and (4) outcomes and consequences—implications of outcomes that affect actors because of a decision. Each chapter concludes with "Stones of Remembrance" to summarize key points and practical applications of concepts learned.

This book aims to engage you, the reader, in a discussion of problem-solving as a life skill, strengthened through guided instruction to reinforce existing competence as a problem-solver and hands-on experiential activities. It addresses the importance of *self* in problem-solving and in responsible decision-making. In today's complex world, these life skills have become vital to ensure our goal as a leader of the free world.

INTRODUCTION

OVERVIEW

The goal of this book is to examine problem-solving use under single-focused and complex settings with the LIBRE (Listen, Identify a concern, Brainstorm, Reality test, Encourage) Model. Problems vary in size and impact. We will discuss problem-solving basic principles, referencing the Castillo-Mendoza clan, who lived in Mexico in the late 1800s, to illustrate their practical application. Their journey is a good example of methodically confronting challenges through problem-solving and collaborative decision-making. This journey is a historical recounting of their rich problem-solving experiences, and their legacy will live for as long as the family keeps it alive. Access to this experience-based wisdom has broadened our understanding of how to approach straightforward and complex problems.

These problem-solving and responsible decision-making stories powerfully illustrate this one family's enlightened responses to the crises. The advantage for us, as readers, is that the selected families set the tone and offered examples of their (1) problem-solving outcomes, (2) values, beliefs, ethics, and assets, and (3) ownership in managing problems. Events and documents support their decision-making wisdom and have become a reference we use to help us with our daily life challenges. Furthermore, following their family journey allows us the space to reflect and document their value to all family members. The "Stones of Remembrance" is that section in this book that represents a repository of their legacy and wisdom. The stones are organic symbols of lasting and significant thoughts, memories, and experiences, which have been documented as jewels of

From Problem-Solving to Responsible Decision-Making,
pp. xi–xvi
www.emeraldgrouppublishing.com

knowledge shared across generations. All other details are in oral history narratives. Acknowledging these limitations offers a perspective when presenting a series of problem-solving events. Their journey is an inventory of defying challenges and the methodically designed strategies generated through strategic problem solving and collaborative decision-making. The historical recounting casts a net of mind-body-spirit knowledge and wisdom suitable for the young, old, and the community.

Five tenets frame problem-solving as a thoughtful process that can involve one or groups of individuals, acting singularly or in community with others. These tenets include: (1) Each person is a unique agent with a specialized life that aligns with the person's skills, experiences, and assets. This person has talents, skills, and the freedom to change, which are characteristic of normal cognitive functioning and self-awareness. Although some people may have never considered themselves change agents, they, in fact, unknowingly play that role daily. As such, what do you see? A compliant, easy-going person whose flexibility capitulates or adjusts to accommodating other people? You manage your actions, thinking, and being accordingly.

As you read this book, consider the cognitive function and mental skills necessary to problem-solve in a systematic and organized way. (2) We all come from a family or unit of people who contribute to who we are becoming and who we are today. (3) We cannot underestimate the importance of community. Living, learning, and accommodating communities supply information about how to live. In watching others and how to solve problems, we learn about life, the good, the bad, and the unstated experiences. (4) Over time, we develop patterns in managing ourselves with the challenges and problems we face. We develop an appreciation of self and expound on our unique traits, skills, and temperaments. (5) The person you are or aspire to be is associated with values defined in daily living and in problem-solving. As we look at challenges and their management through a deliberate and distinct lens, we will see problem-solving approaches from different viewpoints. We stress the importance of "responsible decision-making" as key to complex problem-solving events. It refers to a collaborative approach managed by groups to address complex problems. Corporate businesses have boards of directors to help manage such concerns. We, too, could benefit by seeking the wisdom of others with more specialized expertise. At the end of most chapters, "Stones of Remembrance" provides interactive exercises to apply these principles in real-life scenarios.

Following reflection, readers review their conflict management strategy and complete plans for brainstorming and reality-testing proposed solutions and their consequences. The book's organization consists of three sections: Section I: Problem-Solving, Section II: Responsible Decision Making, and Section III: You and Your Journey.

Section I: Problem-Solving

The first section consists of five chapters. Chapter 1, "The Story Begins" invites the reader to join and partner in our journey throughout the book.

The Castillo and Mendoza families are the key actors in this historical journey that happened as Spain offered land grants to settle in the New World. Our unleashed imagination captured the intriguing and harsh life of these families that sought a better life in a more conducive environment. Reference to actual occurrences, documentation from family events, oral histories, legal documents, and church files provide evidence of historical significance. The book focuses on family inferences behind the scenes and discussions intended to support text concepts. Extended-living family members who may one day read this book will appreciate this caveat. This chapter presents events to help us ponder problem-solving as a life skill.

Chapter 2, "Self and Identity in Problem-Solving," examines a person's various roles in the problem-solving exchange. The chapter presents three developmental theories that examine self-awareness, social awareness, and self-management. Furthermore, it discusses self—the "who we are" and identity" the groomed self, who we are becoming" to set the stage for the presentation of developmental considerations in conflict management. Examined are daily challenge occurrence(s) and responses found in everyone's life that reflect "who we are" and "a groomed response." The chapter closes with definitions of self-in-identity, descriptions of what makes up a problem, and the basic ingredients in problem-solving. "Stones of Remembrance" supplies space to consider lessons learned and any potential takeaways.

Chapter 3, "When Challenge Occurs," explores self-in-identity as critical to identifying challenges or problems. We briefly discuss how we naturally want our base to be calm. Identity—who we are becoming—offers space to consider conflict management. Like most problems, conflict is often associated with social exchange, involving oneself and other aggrieved people(s). For instance, the person who says, "If I am doing what I want, when I want, as I want, then there is no problem." The chapter discusses approach/avoidance tendencies and personal crisis management as articulated through Erikson's stages of development (Erikson, 1963) and Maslow's hierarchy of needs (Maslow, 1968). The chapter closes with a discussion of crisis resolution implications and with the "Stones of Remembrance."

Chapter 4, "Strategy for Addressing the Problem," discusses the LIBRE (Listen, identify a concern, Brainstorm, Reality-test, Encourage) Model (Guerra, 2015, 2016) and LIBRE Model Engagement styles (Guerra, 2006, 2009b). Self-awareness and self-management are developmental qualities that individuals develop through life experiences and social affordances.

The chapter closes with a discussion of the problem-solving process and "Stones of Remembrance."

Chapter 5, "Reflections on Problem-Solving," examines the gains and losses associated with a straightforward problem-solving approach as it affects self and community. There is a discussion on the importance of the human development process, crisis management, hierarchical physiological, psychological, and social needs, ecological, and engagement styles. The chapter closes with a discussion on the critical role of self, self-awareness, and the whole person. "Stones of Remembrance" reviews lessons learned.

Section II: Responsible Decision Making

This section, Chapter 6, "The Story Continued," outlines additional Castillo-Mendoza events using the following framework: What is involved in solving complex challenges? Who wins or loses in problem-solving? What role does the community play in brainstorming and selecting workable solutions? "Stones of Remembrance" closes the chapter.

Chapter 7, "Responsible Decision-Making: Context and Relational Climate," examines the value of self as an integral part of a community. Environmental cues provide valuable information for managing oneself and others. The focus is on community values and individual self-identity. Kaufman's (2020) examines and explores self-actualization and its connection to whole-person principles. The problem-solving event equally emphasizes self and context when considering a problem. The chapter closes with "Stones of Remembrance," a collection of personalized takeaways.

Chapter 8 examines "Responsible Decision-Making: The Identified Concern." The questions explored include: How does one become a whole person? How does one balance one's needs in the community without losing oneself or sacrificing identity? Consider when and where to acknowledge *self* within the problem-solving exchange. The problem solver must be an integral part of the problem-identification process. The "Stones of Remembrance" include self-reflection activities and lessons learned.

Chapter 9, "Processing Responsible Decision-Making: Brainstorming and Reality-Testing," discusses a problem-solving approach, specifically through a self-actualized lens (Guerra, 2016), emphasizing community-based brainstorming and reality-testing of solutions. The chapter concludes with an introduction to the last step of the LIBRE Model, Encouragement, which is the planned resolution stage. A mantra statement embodies the lesson learned from the exchange and reinforces the value of the collaborative-based resolution. This discussion also captures the essence of ecological layering on the development of the resolution plan. "Stones of Remembrance" stresses the importance of lessons learned.

Section II: Chapter 10 "Responsible Decision-making: Encouraged to Plan," opens with a revisit to the question, What is involved in responsible decision making? We discuss the differences between straightforward problem-solving and collaborative decision-making. This chapter challenges us to reflect on personal and communal growth. We consider these questions: "Who contributes to the developed shared values in the community?" "What are your lived values," "Do your values fit you?" "Do your values fit your self-identity? "Have you allowed yourself space to grow?" "Does your self-identity fit in your community?"

A combination of self and community and the best of self and the best of community in addressing challenges is at the crux of problem-solving. The integrated investment of both (self and community) is necessary to face complex challenges. Just to remind ourselves that self and social awareness are the foundation to effective problem-solving. "Stones of Remembrance" invites us to consider takeaway lessons.

Section III: You on Your Journey

The book concludes by reflecting on the Castillo-Mendoza story, examining the problem-solving results and feedback from the descendants who relocated to Texas for a fresh start.

Chapter 11, "From Problem-Solving to Responsible Decision-Making: Stones of Remembrance," examines the role of key markers in the LIBRE Model decision stages that support problem-solving efficacy. We reinforce the idea that Erikson's life span model is a framework for communities to reevaluate self-in-identity as human growth and development as central in the problem-solving and responsible decision-making processes. We review self-in-identity in community as an integral part of human growth and development. Proposed is a problem-solving approach that shows the intersection of self-actualized "best of you" with the self-actualized "best of community" when considering complex challenges. The chapter invites readers to explore their personal history and family narratives when facing problems. "Stones of Remembrance" space allows the reader to organize the chapter's takeaways.

Chapter 12, "My Family Responsible Decision-Making Experience," provides intentional space to create and document mission, goals, and accomplishments. To offer an example, the author begins with her story.

Consider the prompts given that address context, ecological and crisis-oriented development, and intersectionality of self, as a whole person in a community. The significance of self, as a whole person contributing to the community, values developed with others, and extended systems offer an opportunity to identify values associated with crisis management. In others, we learn from past problem-solving experiences—what worked and what was ineffective and aligned with our shared values. Networking bolsters skilled people's ability, and their wisdom informs the collaborative problem-solving process. Furthermore, it is an advantage that increases the impact of responsible decision-making. "Stones of Remembrance" offers lessons learned for potential takeaways. The intersectionality of past and present family "pláticas" involves more than exchanging stories; they were forums for deep discussions around values to forge a better life. They addressed the consequences of decisions made to face pressing and managing life challenges. Who made the problem-solving decisions, and who benefited from the resolutions? From historical and notable events, people, and opportunities, we learned how diversity of values and beliefs affected decisions that had an impact on life for generations.

The chapter provides lessons applicable today; the historical examples were to inform future decision-making processes. We present the LIBRE Model with questions to frame and present a narrative to practice problem-solving exchanges.

SECTION I

PROBLEM-SOLVING

CHAPTER 1

THE STORY BEGINS

Spain's colonization efforts extended to Florida and Mexico by the 1800s. The Spanish government offered land grants to lure and motivate settlers to inhabit these new lands. The Castillo family, Nicomedes and Felipa, was one of those families. Leaving Spain, they embarked on a journey to Mexico to begin their new life together as a young couple on their claimed land grant near Matehuala, Mexico. Their unwavering faith was steadfast that, without a resolute belief in God, they would not have endured the hardships of the move. Their strong faith and religious beliefs influenced every aspect of their lives. They were devoted parents who welcomed their two daughters and catered to them, providing a good environment and education. The Castillos understood the importance of handwork and building trusting relationships and, using their baking skills they mastered in Spain, opening a bakery they named *Rizo de Oro* (Golden Curl or Strand). This business title was significant for their family, serving as their signature branding and business identity. With the family expanding and their survival relying on it, they started baking pan (translated to English means bread).

Moreover, every family member joined the business. Their business was booming; the need for more help became clear. They hired workers to help them deliver their baked goods to other communities. The Castillo parents wanted to ensure that their girls played an active role in the daily business and were well protected. They ensured escorts went with them everywhere they went. One of the young men hired was Teodosio Mendoza, a courteous individual with strong farming skills and a shared work ethic. Over time, they proved to have a trusting relationship. Teodosio became

From Problem-Solving to Responsible Decision-Making,
pp. 3–8
www.emeraldgrouppublishing.com

the head ranch manager and had duties that included escorting the Castillo daughters to town, school, and other social events. The family business ran well for many years. The two Castillo girls also grew to become young misses. During this time, Teodosio (affectionately called Teo) showed his prowess and loyalty to the Castillo family as a trusted, valued community member. Teodosio brought his farming skills to the family and began to grow vegetables on their land.

What Was Teo's History?

Teo was born into a blended family. A Texas family named Zuniga had adopted Teo's father as a young boy. While his father never changed his surname from his birth-given name, Mendoza, his father, grew up understanding the importance of family, trust, community, and the value of arduous work. As a young adult, his father married a woman who had previously married and had a son from that relationship. With this new union, Teo's father did not discriminate between his two sons; only Teo was his father's son by blood. Years later, Teo would remain close to his blended family of origin, and he invited this brother (and his family) to move with his family years later.

Where Was the Problem?

Augustina (affectionately called Tina), the younger Castillo daughter, and Teodosio fell in love. This young couple faced their first life challenge; they were in love and wanted to be together. Teo was ready to commit; Tina was five years his junior. They struggled, in their brainstorming, to produce the best solution. They knew her parents would encourage them to wait, but they did not want to delay. Instead, they crafted a straightforward solution. They would go to the courthouse, get married, and return to her family to inform them of their decision to be together as a married couple and with a new family. Thus, they resolved their challenge and moved forward with their developed plan. They left in the morning and returned home in the afternoon as husband and wife. Fortunately, the Castillo parents graciously accepted their decision and welcomed them home.

Tina's parents knew that the couple loved each other, and while they would have preferred a different solution, they understood. The Castillo parents created a home for the young Mendoza couple on their property. Teo had his aspirations, but now, as a new member of the Castillo clan, he knew he would keep his work commitments for and with the Castillos. He continued to help distribute bread products from the Rizo de Oro enterprise, knowing his farming skills were growing corn, okra, and other vegetables. The two families, Castillo and Mendoza, continued to live on Castillo hacienda. The families supported each other and held strong family values for church, culture, and community. They lived by their faith and were active community participants. The assets they embraced included truth, resilience, faith, and respect. With hard work and responsible decision-making, they experienced increased success with the land crops and the bakery businesses, but with time comes change.

Tina and Teo grew the numbers in their family; they now have land in Texas. Teo had met other farmers who told him that he needed to buy land with that many sons. With his wife's agreement, Teo began investing in Texas farming land. Teodosio's self-awareness and assuredness in his farming skills gave him a sense of empowerment. This straightforward decision involved only Teo and Tina. With her love and support, they bought land in Texas, knowing that potential change and entrepreneurship could change their close relationship as a family. These purchases suggested independence and a deviation from the Castillo family bakery business.

Meanwhile, by 1910, Mexico was in a state of disruption, experiencing economic, political, and civil unrest. The Revolution War of 1910 was underway. Pancho Villa appeared as an activist and a revolutionist. Teo and Tina Mendoza's 11 sons were now young men entering adulthood. Soon, they would marry and venture out to set up their life pathways. The Mendoza parents felt a deep sense of unease and worry about the safety and political instability in Mexico. Unfortunately, their feared concern became a reality in 1913. The straightforward crisis became a single-focused problem when their 16-year-old son made a spontaneous decision. While making his regular deliveries, their son ran into Pancho Villa and his men. Pancho Villa was passionate in his belief that people experiencing poverty did not deserve abuse by politicians; people experiencing poverty must fight for their God-given rights, and his message was clear: this was the time ripe for revolution.

Young Mendoza listened to Pancho Villa speak and became enamored with the powerful message to support human equality and adventure. At that moment, young Mendoza saw an opportunity to join this revolutionary cause. He instructed his accompanying workers and bodyguards to return and inform his parents that he would not return home; instead, he decided to join Pancho Villa and the revolutionary cause. The workers returned to the hacienda and relayed the message.

According to oral historical accounts, Augustina was the first to receive the message. She notified her husband. Teodosio returned home at once. He knew his son's decision had created a challenge that could alter their lives forever. His son's immediate danger, juxtaposed with his son's courage and commitment to a value-laden cause.

He feared his son was in immediate danger and sought an expedited decision. Teodosio was fully aware of his responsibility to provide his children with life experiences that prepared them to live through good and perilous times. He, with his wife by his side, had to find a solution that would minimize the danger and enrich his son's adventurous spirit with experiences to become more adroit in facing life and societal problems. The Mendoza family saw the existing larger environmental dangers and changes around them. They knew they were facing a dilemma: overprotecting their children from societal vicissitudes or allowing them to become adults skillfully groomed in problem-solving personal, community, and societal challenges that they would eventually face. The family examined the problem's contextual considerations and identified the problem: "how do we retrieve our son as quickly as possible?" The brainstorming began. One can only assume that Teodosio and Augustina sat at their kitchen table to consider the "how" and "when." As they began to assess options, they consulted the workers who could lead him back to the Villa camp. They said, "yes," encouraging action. He and his wife prepared the strategic plan that called for an immediate but carefully crafted element of surprise to get him out safely. They were encouraged as they identified actions with timelines and decided that it all had to occur without delay. The element of surprise and their faith were their strengths to regaining their son. Teodosio, taking several of his trusted workers, approached the Villa camp. Once they arrived, Teodosio approached his son; they quickly embraced, and without delay, they all returned home. There was a celebration in the home that evening with prayers for thanksgiving.

APPLIED SOCIAL AND EMOTIONAL SKILLS TO RESPONSIBLE DECISION MAKING (RDM)

This section has four objectives: (1) assess important mind-body-spirit/ whole person decisions made by these ancestors to show how these decisions affected their lives and study the processes and tools they used to reach the best possible decisions; (2) cite the literature that defines the cognitive, emotional, and sociological perspectives and underpinnings that support effective and efficient problem-solving as decision-making processes; (3) use the important decisions made by our ancestors to show how the cognitive, emotional, and sociological perspectives were considered in reaching responsible decisions; and (4) provide the reader with opportunities to experience problem-solving, including the importance of context, identification of the problem, brainstorming and reality-testing solutions and consequences, and the encouragement in creating a resolution/implementation plan.

Folkman (2021) followed approximately 47,000 men and 24,000 women to report a special acumen in their ability to problem-solve. He asserted, "8 Consistent Behaviors of Practically Perfect Problem Solvers," that he called, *360-degree assessments*. Through interviews, peer reports, work peer reports, and observations, he reported evidence that men tend to outperform women in technical expertise/acumen (T-Value 2.276, Sig. 0,023), and women tend to outperform men in the problem-solving exchange (T-Value 2.432, Sig. .015). The study concluded that women outperformed men in the following competencies or behaviors described by category that define "practically perfect problem-solvers":

1. Self-awareness: takes greater initiative to succeed in problem-solving exchanges;
2. Self-management: shows great potential and truly a role models;
3. Social awareness: invites cooperation of teams in achieving objectives;
4. Relational skills: models and communicates direction and purpose;
5. Self-management: perceptive and quick in identifying problems;
6. Social awareness: inspires people to give their best;
7. Responsible decision-making: goal focused;
8. Social awareness: partners with others to understand the context of a problem;
9. Relational skills: sought after by peers for advice and counsel; and
10. Self-awareness: shares analytic mind with peers.

These self-awareness, social awareness, self-management, relational skills, and responsible decision-making literatures support the bridge between human development and *self* to inform the problem-solving and decision-making processes. Bandura (1986) presents the person as an agent who manages social cognitive development influences to life events. Thus, social cognitive development influences and informs the individual's applied problem-solving development and competencies.

Cognitive, behavioral, and environmental interactions influence the self-agency and directional experiences. For example, a young boy communicating with his father in a potentially dangerous setting involving sheets of metal. The father indignantly shouts, "Pay attention!" When they return to the ground, the father quips, "How many nails do you think we will need to hold the metal down? Get the nails." Over time, and with earlier experiences (of having to return back and forth for nails), he learns to pay attention to the details, check for safety, and make precise calculations when securing sheet metal nails. He now knows how many nails it takes to meet the task efficiently. The young man creates a personal remembrance, a mantra, a phrase designed to support his learned investment. "I am a smart person," he reflects, "I have this."

STONES OF REMEMBRANCE

Values and beliefs define who we are and who we are becoming. Amidst the backdrop of social upheaval, the Castillo and Mendoza families successfully processed their challenges by adhering to their principles. They lived as individuals and as a family, respectful of themselves and offering that same respect to others. For the Castillo and Mendoza families, church, culture, community, and trusting relationships were core values observable in their daily work, individual problem-solving, and family decision-making. Self-awareness, self-management, and social management, and understanding of relational skills served them well in their complex exchanges as individuals, family, and in community.

CHAPTER 2

SELF AND IDENTITY IN PROBLEM-SOLVING—LISTENING AND LEARNING OF SELF

Our problem-solving journey begins with a closer look at social context in relation to self, others, and the value of community in social development (Guerra et al., 2024). We focus on who we are (self and identity) and how we develop and change. Fundamental factors contributing to a skilled problem-solver include a self-awareness to invest and a commitment to learn, grow, change in the middle of managing a problem. A word of caution: Beware! Fear can appear as an unwillingness to take risks, or a paralyzing feeling of helplessness. If this occurs, there is a diminished urgency that can lead to a point of inactivity, affecting important decisions. Proposed is the LIBRE Model, which records personal growth development in approaching a problem and in addressing the challenge through planning and structured conflict resolution strategies toward potential solutions. Let us consider a young man as an example. He is afraid of what others may think of him. He reasons that he will remain unchanged, ignoring investments in his human development, and an exiting problem. This decision may provide immediate convenience for him or others who do not want him to change. The disservice to himself is found as a loss in self-management. Self-reflection and investment invite people to listen and learn about where and who they are as they move from one setting or context to another. Self-investment paves the way for social investments, fostering a broader exploration of perspectives, values, priorities, and experiences for both

From Problem-Solving to Responsible Decision-Making,
pp. 9–22
www.emeraldgrouppublishing.com

oneself and others. Self-reflection invites self-discovery. Let us begin with key working definitions:

1. **What is a problem?** A problem is a predictable or unforeseen life obstacle leading to a welcomed or unwanted consequence. A problem can be personal, group-related, and/or layered with one or more events. For the skilled problem-solver, a challenge holds life-altering opportunities to self-reflect on alternative solutions with multiple change consequence scenarios.

2. **What constitutes a problem?** An interruption of routinized events, a work-related conflict, or socially engineered conflicts that create a need for problem-solving strategies, generating actionable or unfair consequences.

3. **How are problems and problem-solving linked to "self" and "identity" development?** Problems arise from personal and social interactions or events requiring various degrees and types of change. The formulation and experience of daily living immersed in a problem prone environment involves emotions of self and identity. Self-awareness is often the unstated variable in addressing a problem. To address a problem, people must engage self-in-relation to the problem-solving typified by their sense of identity. For example, young children who have not had the chance to practice problem-solving exchanges during their development stages tend to have limited problem-resolution skills during their adolescent and adult lives. Their understanding and strengthening of a sense of self, identity, and self-awareness will be instrumental and influential in the development of an effective and efficient problem-management style.

4. **Why is problem-solving skill development important?** Problem-solving is a life skill. The problem-solving skill develops in the culmination of learned and practiced processes, including naming/identifying a problem, reflecting, brainstorming, reality-testing in order to deduce need and develop resolution action-planning to introduce personal self-exploration. The willingness to study the change and learn problem-solving processes allows for increased self-awareness and management.

5. **What is the difference between problem-solving and responsible decision-making?** Problem-solving is a singularly managed straight-forward exchange to a challenge. For instance, "What am I going to have for dinner?" "What do I already have to in the refrigerator that I can use to prepare for dinner?" "If I go out to each, how much will I have to pay for dinner?" Because I am preparing the meal for myself, the problem-solving focus is on what I want to

eat, what I have in the refrigerator, along with how much I am willing to invest in that meal.

6. **What is responsible decision-making?** For this book, responsible decision-making is associated with a complex problem-solving event. Responsible decision-making refers to problem-solving conducted collaboratively to address a complex problem. An example is the preparation for a large dinner. Some guests have special dietary restrictions. For example, young people have distinct eating sensitivities, and others have specific eating preferences. Problem complexity and outcome impact make responsible decision-making an ideal approach. The outcome impact is consistent with the number of actors affected by the nature of the problem, ecological challenges, and solution complexity. Problem-solvers (PS) address the larger environmental challenge by examining implications through outcome planning and development. The feature of a multiple problem-solvers approach requires all PSs to brainstorm and develop alternative solutions, which will trigger the reality-testing of solution options. This approach ensures a maximum "win" resolution to address multiple PS needs. The outcome impact is consistent with the number of actors affected by the problem's nature, ecological challenges, and the complexity of the solution. PSs address the implications of the problem to the larger ecological systems through outcome planning and development interventions. The feature of a multiple problem-solvers approach requires all PSs to brainstorm and develop alternative solutions, which will trigger the reality-testing of solution options. This approach ensures a maximum "win" resolution to address multiple PS needs. With this PS example, all guests enjoy eating the food served. In summary, problem-solving, and responsible decision-making approaches frame complex problems, describe the multiple needs of PSs, and define the implications of the solutions' imbued consequences. The more aware and informed problem solvers become, the more likely they are to access resources and skilled support to resolve complex problems.

Several targeted human development theories are introduced to explore a problem-solver's self-development to change and challenge the impact of learning and growing while becoming proficient in the problem-solving exchange. This presentation helps set the stage for us to consider the differences suggested in examining individual and group management of a problem-solving event.

Self and Identity Within the Listen and List Prompt

Investment in self and identity is pivotal to understanding problem-solving as a living, learning, growing, and developing experience. To be effective at problem-solving, one must regularly assess one's social and personal identity. This cyclical reflection is between you and your environment. The focus is on changes to self, personal interactions, responses, and problem-solving helps one learn more about self and identity as an influential factor affecting the quality of change or solution exploration you are willing to consider. As one is becoming more proficient as a problem-solver, there are multiple re-visits to where you have been and where you are going with your thinking, values, and beliefs. You will want to take note of how you respond in one setting as opposed to another. You may feel very confident with persons you know but find yourself less willing to speak-up with persons that are recent acquaintances.

In this section, we examine how self and identity within the context of the problem influences the problem-solving process. Is "self" different from "identity?" *Self* is like a unique fingerprint, with distinct features, biological traits, and temperament.

Identity influences the management of intentional and unintentional transitions in the development process. Teodosio's use of observation, intelligence, adaptability, and desire to learn is a prime example of self-incorporated development. His family background, experiences, and values influenced Teodosio's identity. The early and formative life of Teodosio's father, which included his adoption and upbringing by another family, alerted him to the value of a traditional family. As a child, Teodosio's family included a sibling, a half-brother from his mother's earlier marriage. Teodosio's family was engaging, and work was a robust prevailing ethic from an early age. Thus, change, problem-solving, and adaptability were backdrops to Teodosio's father and his development.

Teodosio looked up to his father, who emphasized the significance of the family unit, and aimed to be an industrious individual like him. Teodosio's biological, cognitive, *self-identity*, behavioral, and social skills shaped his development as an industrious person. Viewing *self* and *identity* through the lens of intersectionality involves considering how biological assets and life experiences intersect. The way Teodosio interacts with others defines his sense of self and *identity*. *Self* is the result of his biological assets; *Identity* is the culmination of life's formative experiences and the influences on his behavior that define who Teodosio became. Conversely, self (who) and identity (how) define individuals' lives, how they interact with others, and how they manage life and problems.

We have a predisposition to be lifelong learners. The more we invest in learning, the greater our self-awareness and the greater the opportunity for our continued growth and development in becoming skilled prob-lem-solvers (Guerra, 2016). What is the significance of "self and identity" development in problem-solving? Living in a human developmental milieu surrounded by social, cognitive, emotional, and psychosocial events and experiences provides insights into how we manage ourselves and our problems (American Psychological Association, 2017).

SOCIAL, COGNITIVE, EMOTIONAL, AND PSYCHOSOCIAL DEVELOPMENT

Self and Identity Within Context

Our childhood and adolescent experiences have a lasting impact on self-identity development. We form connections with individuals in our surroundings whom we either admire, respect, and hold in high regard, or despise, disrespect, and hold in contempt, creating positive or nega-tive emotional attachments. These people include our parents, siblings, extended family members, and community members. Their impact can be positive or have an adverse and detrimental effect on self and identity development. The goal is to have experiences that promote a heightened sense of *self and identity*. When we are young, we know outright, groomed, or suggested, "what to and not be," often embracing judgments reflect-ing parents' or caregivers' values, culture, and community standards. The parents' and caregivers' self-awareness and healthiness may introduce factors that potentially affect self and identity. For example, the egocentric father who wants his son to be an extension of him. This dynamic will influ-ence the son's identity development.

During adolescence, self-awareness becomes a critical hurdle, according to Miller (2011) who referred to it as a painful stage. We now speak for ourselves, trying to fit in and formalize self and identity. The aim is not to look different from the cool kids and manage to fit in. The journey of life includes change as a fact, obstacles, and conflicts. Before we realize it, we have developed an identity incorporating the simplicities and complexities of life generated through childhood and adolescent experiences. Ado-lescents often struggle with the unpredictability of behavior, alternating between mature and childish choices. The young Mendoza's adventure is a good example of this challenge.

In Summary

Problem-solving is adaptive to match human developmental changes. Self and social awareness are essential for individuals to function as agents, taking responsibility for their own *identity* (Bandura, 2000). For example, young Mendoza had a protected and privileged life. His social community supported his freedom to explore and protected him. Roles of *self* and *identity* influence internal changes related to problem-solving efficacy.

SELF AND IDENTITY IN COMMUNITY

Bronfenbrenner (1989) explains that individual development is an ecological system. Biological, social, and environmental connections shape and influence our lives and ambiance. Available opportunities provide individuals important information. The shrinking life experiences of Augustina and Teodosio exemplify how differing life opportunities influenced their ecological identity development. Augustina's family was more privileged than Teodosio's. She had better opportunities to meet her basic needs. She did not have to work for survival andgrew up with servants and the security of a protected community. Teodosio's family was "blended;" his mother's second marriage, different socioeconomic status, and half-brother made his family's ecological system non-traditional and different. He grew up influenced by his father's persevering work ethic and family values.

Bronfenbrenner (1989) used a nested doll analogy to describe the distinct ecological levels between the dolls and explained how the transitional phenomenon led to ecological self and identity development. He posits that four contextual levels influence development and identity. At the most basic level is the *microsystem*, which includes "patterns of activities, roles, and interpersonal relations experienced by the developing person in a given face-to-face setting," including the nurturing provided at home by parents and family. As the individual develops, the *mesosystem* offers extended "linkages and processes that take place between two or more settings within the developing person." Examples include attending school or church. As the individual reaches the *exosystem*, "links and processes take place between two or more settings, at least one of which does not ordinarily contact the developing person." For instance, social exchanges, like those that occurred as Teodosio traveled between communities. He learned to collaborate with different people, cultures, and languages. He left his family of origin to find a new path for himself, using the farming and communication skills he had learned. The fourth ecological system is the macrosystem, which is an "overarching pattern of micro-, meso-, and exosystem characteristics of a given culture, subculture, or other broader social contexts." Bronfenbrenner clearly articulated that these systems functioned as networks of development for specific values and beliefs, leading to identity.

The Castillo family and faith influenced Teodosio's identity development; they were devout Catholics and attended church regularly. Their faith was foundational to how they raised their family. Records show that their faith was consistent and repeatedly supported. Years later, the Mendoza family continued to give of their first crop to the church in gratitude and thanksgiving. Their church affiliation changed, but their collective identity continued to develop experientially and reflected their assumed decisions and problem-solving. The family could have invested their gains differently but instead lived unpretentiously aligning their problem-solving to their values.

In Summary

The development of self and identity does not occur in isolation or apart from personal and social exchanges. In fact, identity development continues from birth to adolescence to adulthood. These exchanges are important and play a notable role in the rearing of the Castillo and Mendoza families.

SELF AND IDENTITY IN SOCIAL AND EMOTIONAL LEARNING

Bandura (1986) explains that identity development involves a social cognitive exchange, influenced by the reciprocity of the environment, behavior, and the self. His developmental view is that self and identity are artifacts of a socialization process involving interactive reciprocal exchanges between the person, their behavior, and the environment, in such a way that development occurs (Bandura, 2000). Teodosio's personal are an example of how they intertwined with his farming orientations in Mexico and Texas. His diligent behavior and personal ethic resulted from learned and groomed experiences gained from his father and reinforced while he moved from job to job. As an agent of self, he actively pursued what he wanted to be and do with his life. While Bandura did not articulate development with the same ecological lens as Bronfenbrenner (1989), Bandura, too, saw identity as a social exchange.

The Collaborative for Academic, Social, and Emotional Learning (SEL) developed what it refers to as the SEL rubric which includes five distinct skills that contribute to identity development (CASEL, 2003). These skills include *self-awareness*, which refers to one's attentiveness to self, social awareness to a person's conscious attention to others; and *self-management* to a person's skills to control self, and one's behavior, emotions, and work habits toward a productive outcome in private, professional, and social settings. *Relational skills* refer to skills that help interpersonal and interactive exchanges in social settings yield positive results. Finally, responsible decision-making ensures that inclusive problem-solving provides a positive return for all involved individuals/events. Self-awareness, social awareness, and relational skills influence self-management of efficient problem-solving. Bandura (1997) explained that self-efficacy (an individual's predisposition to succeed) is related to the successful processing of information and acting with the confidence to succeed.

The Mendoza family illustrates how they created initiative pathways for their 11 sons and 1 daughter as they traveled from town to town, delivering bread and vegetables. Augustina had been a businessperson delivering bread and had the freedom to travel in the surrounding communities. Her children received these benefits, which led to greater self-efficacy in negotiating. These experiences nurtured their confidence and business-minded identity.

In Summary

Learning is not always intentional or directive in development; conversely, incidental learning can have a greater influence on development (Bandura, 1997). For example, young Mendoza, Teodosio's father, while living with a family other than his birth family, learned to adapt, accommodate, and survive primarily through social exchanges. The takeaway is that while we continue to grow, community and social exchanges play a significant role in the development process. Assets do not only come from family, but from those in your immediate environment. Shared values, culture, socioeconomic status, and beliefs also influence our developing identity. An example was the young Teodosio Mendoza family and their social exchanges. Teodosio embraced diversity and opportunities as he moved freely from one country to another, interacting with many diverse communities. Learning positively influences our identity development. Including a need-based model allows us to consider the developmental question: What does one need to live, survive, and thrive?

SELF AND IDENTITY IN MEETING INDIVIDUAL NEEDS

Maslow (1998) developed a hierarchy of needs. Kaufman (2020) working from Maslow's original work (1943), asserted that attainment of a functional self-actualized identity requires success in the preceding developmental stages. The extended thought was that addressing safety needs must occur before the willingness to connect occurs and growth thrives. When an immediate need goes unmet, a distortion may arise in the individual's developmental inclination. Therefore, unmet needs hinder the profound growth or engagement that is foundational to achieving self-actualization. Maslow explained that all people have an ongoing quest to meet their need for self-actualization. Development is an add-on linked to the pace of meeting basic needs. Once a person has met the basic needs prerequisite, new levels of development and new motivational goals are set. The process, enhanced by exploration, now faces a new set of needs. Truncating basic needs decelerates the developmental process. Therefore, meeting self-actualized goals faces a compromised developmental path rather than a "flexibility in repertoire" path. For example, unmet basic needs delay reaching self-actualization goals at the expected time and require extra help and resources to get back on track. Reaching self-actualization becomes the goal and a problem.

Kaufman (2020) continued Maslow's (1943) line of thought by introducing the term "transcendence" to describe the importance of having and supporting a strong and secure foundation to aid growth in personal development. "Purpose" motivates, inspires, allowing ongoing exploration and development of valued life goals. Processed information flows continuously, satisfying basic needs and increasing a person's direction to their defined "goals." For instance, reaching the goal of security (with food) facilitates a motivation to seek a sense of belonging. Each person defines their personal goals. For example, Teodosio had a myriad of goals, acquisitions, and was successful in his journey from safety to belonging, thus helping him reach his goal of achieving self-actualization. He became a farmer, learned to grow vegetables to meet basic immediate needs, and through those investments, he was able to meet other needs that contributed to his overall growth and development.

In Summary

These hierarchy of needs with developmental models challenge the reader to reflect and explore the critical role that identity has in problem-solving efficacy. Information gathered may align, inform, or remain a reflection of the life experiences in defining self and identity as essential constructs of problem-solving. Thus, learning, exploring, and enhancing growth is the goal, not only when problems arise, but continuously as part of everyday living. An explanation of intersectionality, the crossing of self-in-identity, change, and the challenge of human development, will help build a more concise understanding of problem solving.

INTERSECTIONALITY OF
SELF-IN-IDENTITY WITH DEVELOPMENT

We have repeatedly stated that culture, values, and a sense of identity influence the development of the *self*. Life development is perpetual, occurring from birth and adolescence to adulthood until death. Bronfenbrenner (1989) explained the strong bond between the individual and the family, suggesting that both positive and negative family influences are inevitable. Self-awareness is significant to socialization, learning, and development. Augustina grew up and played under the care of her parents. Her experience with the bakery involved social and financial exchanges, giving her full advantage of the opportunities to enhance her identity. She showed how her social awareness and self-management contributed to her success with her family and peers. Augustina managed to satisfy her needs continuously, transcending all boundaries for a woman of her day. Teodosio had a different life, not affluent but with similar arduous work ethics and family values.

Maslow (1943) pointedly addressed the consequences of unmet needs by discussing how that state of mind affects a person. He asserted that an unmet need triggers the urgency and a motivator to get the issue resolved. At some point, an unmet need affects beliefs and creates distortions or triggers defense mechanisms. The person now focuses on protection from the pain generated by a deficiency that truncates growth. Two examples include (1) the hungry person with the unmet goal of food, creating and distorting the normal growth curve; and (2) a person's motivation affected by needing to feel a sense of belonging. In the second example, satisfying an individual's basic needs allows people to pursue the important goals of self-actualization. Individuals who achieve personal self-awareness gains tend to generate investments in their goal of self-actualization. When individuals apply their altruistic self, a willingness to sacrifice for others, and share a deep self-awareness, they have reached self-actualization. Self-awareness and self-management fuse motivation, goals, and purpose and, as Kaufman (2020) suggests, create a new base from which to grow. Bandura's (2000) concept of agency referred to a person capable of achieving their life goals, making choices, and carrying them out.

In Summary

Understanding the complexity of defining who we are and who we are becoming is a challenging undertaking that requires deep thought and reflection. Even if we ponder day and night over an extended period, we have questions about who we are and how we managed to get there. We noted that our values and assets intertwine with our development, beginning at birth and ending with death (Bronfenbrenner, 1989). We also pointed to the concept of socializing that occurs as we see those around us and as we move from place to place. The Castillo-Mendoza family offered a clear picture of life without limits as they moved from home to community and from town to town with their *pan*/bread and produce. Maslow (1998) reminded us that motivation and development are the foundation of self-actualization. Kaufman (2020) added that satisfying needs is the basis from which one grows. This additive value is in being and doing as one navigates from meeting personal needs to extending, exploring, and connecting to be, to do, and offer to others. While we will never have all the information needed to understand self and identity, we know this: we are not alone; we are born in community and influenced by those who surround us. Maslow's shared thoughts on self-actualization offer key takeaways:

- Truth seeking—holds a value and the search for what is true.
- Acceptance—has the willingness to value and appreciate: to engage and receive.
- Purpose—defined direction.
- Authenticity—genuineness and dependability.
- Continued Freshness of Appreciation of and for life, its events, and persons.
- Peak Experiences—attentive to recognizing important or key events.
- Good Moral Intuition—virtuous.
- Creative Spirit—inventive.
- Equanimity—accepting life's difficulties with grace and acceptance (Kaufman, 2020, p. 89).

STONES OF REMEMBRANCE

The focus is on self, the complexity of self-development, and managing substantial amounts of information. Review and assess multiple strategies for developing the whole person. It is important to (1) give yourself space and time to address this development need; (2) reflect; (3) reference sections for future revisits; (4) celebrate positive gains in investment and show yourself grace for the time spent exploring self-development; and (5) ask yourself questions to revisit later or discuss with others. Review what makes your life story unique and contemplate the exchange of information within different settings. Key takeaways include developmental reconsiders (see Table 2.1). This activity is an opportunity to reflect on planning a strategy to address problems or issues from three perspectives in a comprehensive problem-solving mode. The approach capitalizes on Bronfenbrenner's three ecological stages to reflect and document the problem and answer the questions in each of the columns. Study the example provided, select a problem of your choice, reflect on the questions, and document your answers. After completing the exercise share and discuss with a classmate.

Use ecological reflection to help readers structure their thoughts as they process their self-development to solve problems systematically. Table 2.1 offers readers opportunities to examine how self-reflection plays a vital role in problem-solving exchanges at three levels defined by Bronfenbrenner's Ecological System Theory (1979): the microsystem, mesosystem, and ecosystem.

Table 2.1

Activity: Problem-Solving Worksheet to Practice the Application of Self-Reflection in Decision-Making Using Bronfenbrenner's Ecological Systems Theory Which Emphasizes Community

Stage Bronfenbrenner's Ecological System's Theory	Self-Reflections How would you describe experiences that would influence your decision?	Assets (positive support) How would you ensure the dignity of those involved in the problem?	Opportunities (added support to clarify issues) What added support can help address the complexity of the problem?
Microsystem Reflects one's origins upbringing, family, community, and cultural values	Example: • Selecting a life partner is final. About the problem: _____ _____ _____	Example: • Seeking advice from loved ones. About the problem: _____ _____ _____	Example: • Partner is committed and aligned with your philosophy. About the problem: _____ _____ _____

(Table continued on next page)

Table 2.1 Continued

Stage Bronfenbrenner's Ecological System's Theory	Self-Reflections How would you describe experiences that would influence your decision?	Assets (positive support) How would you ensure the dignity of those involved in the problem?	Opportunities (added support to clarify issues) What added support can help address the complexity of the problem?
Mesosystem Links to places outside of home and subcultures (for example, church and the youth group)	Example: Seek advice from priest or pastor re: your decision About the self-selected problem: _____ _____ _____	Example: Consider advice from faith-connected friends re: your problem. About the self-selected problem: _____ _____ _____	Example: Research and read about permanent relationships. About the self-selected problem: _____ _____ _____
Ecosystem Reflects two or more places (for example, work and college; they are distinct or overlapping)	Example: • Share and gather advice and reactions from college friends. About the self-selected problem: _____ _____ _____	Example: • Weigh advice and assess reactions from college friends. About the self-selected problem: _____ _____ _____	Example: • Expand the circle of influencers by seeking professional counseling. About the self-selected problem: _____ _____ _____

(Table continued on next page)

Table 2.1 Continued

Stage Bronfenbrenner's Ecological System's Theory	Self-Reflections How would you describe experiences that would influence your decision?	Assets (positive support) How would you ensure the dignity of those involved in the problem?	Opportunities (added support to clarify issues) What added support can help address the complexity of the problem?
Revisits Space to think and document	Example: • Rethink commitment prior to making final decision. About the self-selected problem: _____ _____ _____	Example: • Reassess pertinent data gathered from all sources when considering final decision. About the self-selected problem: _____ _____ _____	Example: • Finalize commitment to a final decision. About the self-selected problem: _____ _____ _____

This ecological reflection helps you in structuring your thoughts as you begin to process self-development in problem-solving connections. It is important to note that you will likely participate at different levels depending on the setting/context of the community.

CHAPTER 3

WHEN CHALLENGE OCCURS— IDENTIFY A PROBLEM- SOLVING EVENT

SELF-IN-IDENTITY CHALLENGE

Our journey continues, as we now consider challenges a regular part of daily life. Change, like development, does not always occur as a fluid endeavor, but as a " twist and turn " path. Sometimes, we navigate life's intricacies with ease until a "moment of conflict" or developmental challenge arises. As an adolescent, young Mendoza was an example of a time when self-concept (who he was) and his developmental identity took center stage. Identity and experience posed a challenge providing us with an ideal starting point for this inquiry. Is developmental theory reflected in how the individual responds to challenge/problem-solving events? Is there a developmental intersectionality between who young Mendoza was, how he saw himself in this life event, and in the problem-solving experience? If he had been older, would he have responded similarly? First, let us review the developmental path described in Chapter 2 as a unique opportunity to gain experience about the importance of self-development. Bronfenbrenner (1989) and Bandura (1989) introduced the concept of development as a social exchange influenced by ecological systems. In the process, we briefly discussed Maslow's (1943) view of development as dependent on meeting needs. We now shift to Erikson's (1963) crises as the foundation of identity and development. He stressed that identity development occurs through

From Problem-Solving to Responsible Decision-Making,
pp. 23–37
www.emeraldgrouppublishing.com

a series of chronological and psychosocial events occurring from birth to death. Crises in development occur in the person's management of experiences; each stage defines its corresponding identity development as either positive or negative. A person's accumulated prior experience creates objective or prejudiced inclinations from earlier developmental stages that influence future developmental stages. For example, suppose a young child does not receive secure and consistent care from a caregiver. In that case, challenges with trust will appear as a distrust resolution that may, in turn, negatively influence later stages of development.

As a premise for theory development, Erikson's theory also held that developmental expectations were consistent for all people; as such, all follow the same sequenced crisis challenges. Erikson affirmed that each person could resolve life's crisis events as each decided best. Of interest is Erik Erikson's (1959) life span model and his belief that persons resolve with preliminary information and do not "get stuck" in one stage. Erikson's model, influenced by Freud's psychoanalytical theory of development, focuses on crises as developmental response points to address confrontation with change as an additive feature. This crisis point functioned as an open invitation to either continue with the same positive or negative resolve in the earlier stages. The other possibility would be to take a different direction, in this case, by revisiting an earlier stage but this time incorporating added information to change their ongoing developmental experience. Problem-solving opportunities influence human development. Erikson's fluid growth and developmental experiences during his stages of development offer provision to ongoing learning (Erikson, 1963). Erikson (1963) believed that a person could return to an earlier stage of development to self-adjust or reconsider from a former vantage to a new space and change with the added information. For example, the experience with a strict caregiver that occurred early in life engendered mistrust, which can be counteracted or positively resolved by bolstering the level of acquired trust (Evans, 1967). Miller (2011) offers an example: Suppose I learned from guided learning and experiences but lacked initiative in my early development, I can confidently move away from a sense of guilt into an identity of initiative as my resolution.

REFLECTION

One of Erikson's (1963) takeaways is the importance of working, living, learning, and communicating with others. Psychosocial exchanges and communication with others influence each stage of development.

Although Erikson's crisis-management model consists of chronological stages, change may occur when revisiting and reconsidering previous developmental resolutions. He optimistically believed that previous developmental resolutions are subject to change as individuals grow and obtain wisdom through social interactions and learning opportunities. In considering young Mendoza's view of the social exchange with Pancho Villa, Mendoza may not have had the life experience to discern how and when to trust people or look deeper into how to create change without violence.

ERIKSON'S DEVELOPMENTAL STAGES

Erikson (1963) believed that development is sequential, and everyone experiences each crisis stage. Each person experiences each crisis stage in their unique way. Yet, no one experiences or resolves challenges in the same positive or negative way. Whatever the resolution of the "crisis" is, it would carry over to the next stage of development, much like an inclination or weighted experience. Thus, this theory has a cumulative feature. Each stage requires a developmental decision; a crisis point for an individual in the community. No associated ages define Erikson's stages of development, positioning the fluid movement of experiences and influences within each stage to take center stage. To illustrate, each stage has an application example.

Stage 1: Trust Versus Mistrust

This first stage begins with birth. The two polar crisis resolution options available to the newborn include developing trust by meeting basic needs or mistrust due to unmet needs. Considering what this might look like, let us identify a young child looking to her parents or caregivers for the basic needs of food and safety. Meeting these basic needs allows children to gain trust and develop positive inclinations. Similarly, if children receive random or inconsistent care, the inclination to mistrust is a natural part of their development.

Example. Augustina had two parents and multiple caregivers to ensure she had the means to address basic needs. Young Augustina grew up in a supportive and affluent family where the children's needs were a priority and were immediately addressed, always on time. If she cried or needed help, she received it. If she cried or needed help, she had help on hand. Her family and immediate community ensured that she gained trust and confidence, which carried forward into her next stage of development.

Stage 2: Autonomy Versus Shame, Doubt

As growth continues, ongoing communication opportunities intensify. The parents and/or caregivers encouraged the children to take initiative, exposed them to independence, and taught them the function of learned or assumed skills. These experiences demonstrate that the gains obtained in previous stages strengthen and reinforce the development process. Children's formative growth and goals reinforce their self-assessment and identity development. Erikson (1963) explains this as the "hold/let go" stage, where children begin to respond to and with community feedback.

Challenges associated with each chronological stage grow in complexity, and obstacles become more demanding. For example, if children in the first stage fail to get their basic needs met, the takeaway is mistrust. Children who experience negative results in one stage face a difficult transition to the next stage. Erikson's (1963) theory of development provides a stage to assess the impact of both conducive and dysfunctional behaviors on the problem-solving exchange. For example, consider mistrust in individuals who are stuck in the second stage. Will distrustful individuals overcome this handicap? How can they access help? Of equal importance is Erikson's (1963) restorative path, which is the reworking of a development stage until a satisfactory acquisition and performance of a skill as a prerequisite to moving to a higher stage, is an acknowledgement and support of lifelong learning (Miller, 2011). To illustrate, we return to Augustina, who, as a young child, faced the crisis point of embracing autonomy or shame or doubt.

Example. Augustina grew up enjoying the freedom and the space to increase her independence. Her parents and caretakers applauded and celebrated her self-determination. She trusted those around her and developed a sense of self-independence. The security of earlier trusting exchanges and substantial autonomy expedited her development.

Stage 3: Initiative Versus Guilt

Earlier stage resolutions influence Stage 3, specifically the psychosocial exchanges of initiative versus guilt. According to Erikson (1963), a person will automatically progress to the next appropriate chronological stage of development, regardless of the direction assumed in the prior stage. This third crisis point has two directions and considerations: (1) finding an opportunity and taking the initiative to engage to move forward, or (2) identifying a challenge with uncertainty, being indecisive, and feeling guilty for considering action. Guilt is associated with punishment after finding an open space to move to or having moved to that space. The more novel or foreign an experience is, the greater the probability of responding either with an initiative to embrace and invest or to assume self-reproach (guilt) for having considered the initiative. To illustrate, Augustina continued to explore and display initiative.

Example. Augustina's parents modeled and developed confidence by offering her opportunities to be resourceful and to take initiative. They also allowed her a chance to avoid and manage feelings of guilt. Her caregivers encouraged her. Augustina freely went into nearby towns to conduct business, attend church, and visit friends. Her parents wanted to ensure that she continued developing her life skills and confidence. The caregivers were there to assist if she faced a challenge; their role was to protect and be a "safety net" for her.

Stage 4: Industry Versus Inferiority

Erikson (1963) describes *industry* as a "make and complete" stage. Associated with Stage 3 are energy and initiative that provide the motivation, investment, and intentionality to create. On the opposite side of industry is *inferiority*, described as a feeling of inadequacy and self-doubt, a carryover from an earlier stage. Erikson (1963) suggests that this is less than "pretending to" with no investment of energy to improve. Augustina is a strong example of industry.

Example. Young Augustina had initiative and was a determined, active member of her family's bakery business. She was regularly in contact with others inside and outside her family and community. She exemplified the "make and complete" stage with her expression of industry and investment will. She shadowed her older sister, who modeled young women's culturally accepted roles and behaviors.

Stage 5: Identity and Repudiation Versus Identity Diffusion

Establishing strict boundaries can trigger chaos, which we can label erroneously and temporarily disrupt the identity development journey. For example, this stage is a critical and pivotal crisis management point, particularly for adolescents. Individual self-management, interaction with the community, and interpersonal investment are significant during a state of repudiation. How one sees oneself defines identity, while *repudiation* is associated with rejection. Identity *diffusion* suggests a flow of exploration into this new, emerging self, or confusion, leading to chameleon-like behaviors. Openness and freedom are as much a part of a crisis as "to be oneself and to share being oneself" (Erikson, 1963). Our example continues with Augustina and her friends. She not only had her friends, but she also had her sister's friends, even though they were older than her. Those friends, too, helped facilitate Augustina's development in this stage.

Example. Augustina confidently enjoyed the advantage of being the younger sister. Her sister helped her labor through adolescence, while she progressed into her young adult years of development. Augustina was free to go into towns and visit with friends, knowing that her escort would be there to support her. She was secure in her identity as a teen and then as a young woman.

Stage 6: Intimacy and Solidarity Versus Isolation

A search for *intimacy, solidarity*, and *isolation* is at the crux of this stage. The collective accumulation of experiences in these three states of mind and their impact constitute the baseline to devise a personal resolution to strengthen identity development. Achieving intimacy, a movement toward a deeper appreciation for communication and relationships with someone, becomes evident. Solidarity refers to maturity in resolving personal challenges, even after experiencing conflicts in previous stages, and fosters camaraderie as a part of identity development. Erikson (1963) explains *intimacy* as "losing and finding oneself in another" and *isolation* as aloneness, characterized by a reluctance to risk engagement outside of oneself. The resolution of this stage, as with all prior stages, impacts the stage that follows. Augustina is a solid example of *intimacy*.

Example. Augustina, having grown up secure and protected, found herself ready to transition into the stage of intimacy and solidarity, rather than isolation. Her guard was now a boyfriend. She enjoyed the affections they shared. They had fallen in love and found themselves in each other. Teodosio asked her to marry, and rather than asking for her family's blessing, they went to the courthouse. They then returned home as a married couple.

Stage 7: Generativity Versus Self-Absorption

This crisis stage, *intimacy*, and *solidarity* versus *isolation*, strongly focuses on personal resolution and earlier experiences, decisions, and actions taken throughout the person's lifespan. For instance, the individual seeks to create and nurture challenges to invest in others. The orientation gives support and aid in camaraderie. As expected, the cumulative effect of building on prior experiences supports the development of camaraderie among individuals. As the person receives support, the tendency and desire to provide support to others becomes evident. From the opposite crisis position, the individual may select an "it is all about me" direction, again based on earlier life encounters. Individuals tend to become spiteful, claiming that others should also struggle. Self-absorption is perceived as an entitlement. The example follows Augustina's development at this stage.

Example. Augustina's intentionality in helping her immediate and extended family, friends, and associates is *generativity*. Although she is older now, she has consistently experienced support throughout her life and has held this value in helping others. When the family faced a need, she was ready to assist, and when they decided to move, she extended an invitation to others to join them.

Stage 8: Integrity Versus Despair

Erikson's (1963) eighth stage of development is about resolving issues and challenges that have arisen throughout the person's life development. *Integrity* suggests honesty, truthfulness, and trustworthiness. When asked about this specific stage of development, Joan Erikson, Erik's wife, suggested that a better descriptor would have been to be "intact." This descriptor connotes the notion of being a complete self, willing to remain present. This stage is like Maslow's (1943) self-actualization, addressing an appreciation for life from a life-well-lived viewpoint. Conversely, despair speaks about regretting experiences and a lack of goals to guide their identity development. Returning one final time to Augustina, she portrays the intricacies of this integrity stage.

Example. Augustina lived to the age of 98. She remained in her home with her family until she died. She helped and supported her family and became the primary caregiver to one of her son's daughters when the child's mother died at childbirth. Augustina remained active; she lived with her values intact and achieved self-actualization.

APPROACH/AVOIDANCE

Erikson's (1963) human development theory provides two dichotomous value landings and resolutions for each crisis point of development. Applying these opposing positions in problem-solving approaches, we may find similar dichotomous roles in the concepts of "willingness to stay and invest" versus "avoidance of conflict." Augustina was an ideal referent for exploring the more positive aspects of problem-solving and crisis-resolution in development. Two primary reasons for her selection as our primary example include (1) the availability of information from secondary sources and (2) the richness of life outcome inclination along her pathway.

In Summary

Development is a lifelong goal, with options and pathways. We may not always be aware of ourselves, or of the impact of the inclinations that may have been either intentionally or unintentionally learned. However, as Erikson (1963) suggests, life entails a flow and a freedom to process, learn, experience, and revisit so that by the close of life, we find ourselves "intact" and lacking nothing. Table 3.1 provides a visual display to consider revisits to earlier stages of development for additional growth opportunities. Unlike Freud (1955), Erikson's views embody hope and possibility. Erikson is optimistic and believes that growth, learning, and experience create new possibilities. Hope was a powerful force to counteract the effects of a less-than-ideal solution; people could revisit the less-than-optimal resolution that had occurred in a previous stage with opportunities to resolve it and benefit from the revisit.

We ask you to consider inviting a friend or classmate to discuss examples of problems and descriptions associated with Erikson's Stages of Development. Once you have discussed the examples in Table 3.1, review the last five stages and together create examples and share your thoughts with others.

Table 3.1

Reflecting on Erikson's Developmental Stages' Influence and Impact on Problem-Solving Rationale and Exchanges

Erikson's Stages of Development	Examples of Problems Associated with Each Stage	Cite Examples or Problem-Related Experiences With Each of the Stages
Trust vs. Mistrust (Confident vs. Skeptic)	**Trust-building:** Teacher consoles a girl who cries in school. **Mistrust:** A girl cries in school, and no one pays attention.	**Trust-building:** Student hesitates to play in the band; but the band director reassures her that she has talent. **Mistrust:** Student hesitates to play in the band and the band director forces her to join.

(Table continued on next page)

Table 3.1 Continued

Erikson's Stages of Development	Examples of Problems Associated with Each Stage	Cite Examples or Problem-Related Experiences With Each of the Stages
Autonomy vs. Shame & Doubt *(Independence vs. Helplessness)*	**Autonomy:** She feels happy to be in school **Shame & Doubt:** She feels lost with a specific course and does not seek help	**Autonomy:** The student feels lost but asks the teacher and counselor to assist her **Shame & Doubt:** She feels that she is dumb and does not think that anyone can help her
Initiative vs. Guilt *(Resourcefulness vs. Self-reproach)*	**Initiative:** Student feels happy and offers to help others. **Guilt:** Student feels unsure of herself and asks to be released from the expected task performance.	**Initiative:** Volunteers accept challenges when asked by teachers to help. **Guilt:** Parents feel that participation will slow down the project work and refuse to volunteer.
Industry vs. Inferiority *(Organized vs. Inadequacy)*	**Industry:** **Inferiority:**	**Industry:** **Inferiority:**
Identity and Repudiation vs. Identity Diffusion *(Secure vs. Unstable)*	**Identity and Repudiation:** **Identity Diffusion:**	**Identity and Repudiation:** **Identity Diffusion:**
Intimacy and Solidarity vs. Isolation *(Affectionate vs. Low Self-Esteem)*	**Intimacy and Solidarity:** **Isolation:**	**Intimacy and Solidarity:** **Isolation:**
Generativity vs. Self-absorption *(Caring vs. Egocentric)*	**Generativity:** **Self-absorption:**	**Generativity:** **Self-absorption:**
Integrity vs. Despair *(Self-actualized vs. Hopelessness)*	**Integrity:** **Despair:**	**Integrity:** **Despair:**

As we complete this section, we return to Maslow (1943), who considered development as a motivated effort to meet individual basic needs. Maslow did not view development as an age-related process, but as a need-based response. This presentation invites us to consider what and how individual needs may influence development.

MASLOW'S HIERARCHY OF NEEDS

Maslow (1943) believed that we are all motivated to meet immediate needs. This drive begins with the more basic needs, such as security, which, once met, allows for further directional movement across his needs-referenced pyramid. Kaufman (2020) explained that while Maslow described stated needs, these needs-referenced statements' primary intention was to simply describe categories and hierarchical levels of need linked and synchronized with the mental and physical growth sequences. Maslow never wanted the attention given to this hierarchy of needs; he wanted to stress the importance of meeting foundational needs. Individuals could only realize their full potential once needs were met; he wanted us to focus on the process.

In examining this concept, we return to physiological needs, *food, shelter, and safety*. At the next level is belonging and love—a process to which being a member and/or belonging to a larger group is imperative. This stage is followed by esteem—holding the security of the now met needs; there is the desire, want, and motivation to perform and compete, and at the last pivotal processing point is self-actualization—creative generativity that allows for the most altruistic and selfish selves to be motivated and managed accordingly (Maslow, 1962). Maslow believed that development varied as needs were met and as unmet needs continued to create distortions. For example, when food is not present to meet physical need, it creates a focal point of attention as the person continues to develop with focused attention on meeting that unmet physical need.

Kaufman (2020) continued to promote Maslow's (1962) work and thoughts. To provide context to this research endeavor, Kaufman explained how he approached Maslow's family and associates to pick up where Maslow left off with his death. Kaufman found that Maslow had envisioned self-actualization as the beginning of a new, motivated way to live. Our takeaway thought as we ponder Maslow's motivated needs as drives, "At the end of the day, the best way to have a good death is to live a good life" (Kaufman, 2020, p. 238).

Developmental and Behavioral Assets and Constraints That Influence Quality of a Problem-Solving and Responsible Decision-Making Exchange

We define responsible decision-making (RDM) as the complex behavioral artifact of a problem-solving event involving multiple parties. Like all problem-solving, the event begins with examining the context or setting in which the problem is occurring. Second is the identification of the problem or issue of concern. The RDM difference is the time and investment required to process a problem with multiple problem-solvers' agreement. Exploring the shared understanding of the environment, the identified problem, is just the beginning. Once the problem has been clearly identified, the brainstorming and reality-testing of options for viability and appropriateness begins as a complex activity. As diverse thoughts, insights, and opinions are factored into the discussion to select a feasible and practical solution considerations, all must be given an opportunity to speak and respond to the developing options. From these collaborative exchanges, a crafted and encouraging resolution feeds into an implementation plan. The collaborative goal of this RDM problem-solving event is to select and implement an effective solution to a shared problem that meets the needs of all the problem-solvers in the targeted community. A practical and appropriate solution entails reflective and responsible exchange influenced by experience, informational background, age, environment/context, cultural values and beliefs, engagement styles, and internal and external cognitive factors, including self-identity, self-awareness, self-regulation, motivation, emotions, and interpersonal relationships. We refer to these factors as experiential, developmental, and behavioral assets and constraints that affect the nature and quality of options and decisions. Understanding the intersectionality of these factors in structuring a decision is key to interpreting the nature of a particular decision (see Table 3.2). The purpose of the worksheet in Table 3.2 is to show your understanding of Erikson's Stages of Development by discussing with a friend or classmate key experiential and behavioral attributes that affect each step of the problem-solving process.

Table 3.2

Developmental and Behavioral Assets and Constraints That Influence the Quality of a Problem-Solving and Responsible Decision-Making Exchange

Definition of key experiential, developmental and behavioral attributes that affect the quality of decisions	Constructive Influence: How does this asset influence the quality of problem-solving events?	Constraining Impact: When is it a constraint, and how does it influence a decision?
Concept of Self is open and self-reflect to learn and grow	Solutions tend to be creative and innovative, promoting ideas with broad support and impact on all affected persons.	A low concept of "self" means a limited or no understanding of "self" as unique and special. Decisions *are routinely accepted and traditionally bound; solutions lack originality and broad support.*

(*Table continued on next page*)

Table 3.2 Continued

Definition of key experiential, developmental and behavioral attributes that affect the quality of decisions	Constructive Influence: How does this asset influence the quality of problem-solving events?	Constraining Impact: When is it a constraint, and how does it influence a decision?
Concept of Self is open and self-reflect to learn and grow	Solutions tend to be creative and innovative, promoting ideas with broad support and impact on all affected persons.	A low concept of "self" means a limited or no understanding of "self" as unique and special. *Decisions are routinely accepted and traditionally bound; solutions lack originality and broad support.*
Identity is self-actual in awareness, ready to address who one is, what one believes, and what one values/ actions consequences for others.	Solutions reflect a special connection to ensuring all affected individuals benefit from the decision.	A lack of identity attributes externalizes self to descriptions that address skill or other valued persons. Consequently, these problem-solvers implement actions that, left unchecked, can have negative consequences for *others*.
Self-awareness refers to the learned ability to monitor one's thoughts, intuitions, and actions	Solutions tend to be objective and open to innovative ideas.	Decisions are subject to limits due to a closed understanding of self; "I am who I am" but unable and unwilling to reflect and act. Decisions are made without brainstorming options.
Self-regulation refers to a sensitivity and knowledge of "self" and promotes a sense of immediacy in monitoring and managing personal behavior	Solutions tend to be examined thoroughly and assessed using comprehensive criteria.	Decisions reflect a lack of self-awareness and a limited need to regulate behavior. Problem-solvers tend to act impulsively and easily influenced by others.
Self-actualization refers to the point where the individual experiences self as both altruistic and self-oriented.	Problem-solvers feel that no problem is unsurmountable; decisions can be reached by utilizing resources that help craft solutions.	Problem-solvers lack a positive concept of self-regulation, and self-awareness. They tend to feel overwhelmed and move slowly to make critical decisions.

(Table continued on next page)

Table 3.2 Continued

Definition of key experiential, developmental and behavioral attributes that affect the quality of decisions	Constructive Influence: How does this asset influence the quality of problem-solving events?	Constraining Impact: When is it a constraint, and how does it influence a decision?
Informational Background refers to the level of relevant knowledge held by the problem-solver and influencers.	Problem-solvers with a broad knowledge base to support a decision tend to support and augment the brainstorming of options activity.	Problem-solvers with a limited knowledge base tend to dissuade discussion of brainstorming options and limit the number of options.
Cultural values and beliefs are shaped by race and ethnic concepts about life and the role of an individual within the confines of their concept of society. These concepts are engrained in tradition, social norms, and faith, which defines what is right or wrong.	Problem-solvers ensure that decisions respect and honor existing cultural values and beliefs. Decisions are better addressed by individuals who share these beliefs and values.	Problem-solvers who fail to factor cultural values and beliefs in decisions related to specific problems tend to develop and brainstorm irrelevant and dysfunctional solution options that may provide inappropriate resolutions.
Environment/Context refers to the social setting and the context in which a problem emerges.	Problem-solvers' social setting and awareness of what is happening around them	Social setting and no awareness of what is happening around you
Engagement Styles refer to preferred ways of social engagement and processing information. The LIBRE Model describes four styles: actual, goal-focused, venting, and potential.	Problem-solvers address complex problems and utilize a collaborative approach, benefit by not limiting the participation of partners and influencers in sharing critical data that informs the decision-making process. This involves respect and an invitation to entertain contributions by respecting and factoring in different engagement styles.	A lack of awareness of diverse ways to engage in problem definition, resolution options, and solution selection tends to limit the potential to hear diverse viewpoints and limit participation by key influencers who will shy away.

(Table continued on next page)

Table 3.2 Continued

Definition of key experiential, developmental and behavioral attributes that affect the quality of decisions	Constructive Influence: How does this asset influence the quality of problem-solving events?	Constraining Impact: When is it a constraint, and how does it influence a decision?
Social Awareness refers to the learned expertise to self-monitor in settings that include groups of persons.	Problem-solvers with social awareness skills tend to provide leadership, particularly in complex problem solutions where groups of influencers participate in deliberations and problem-solving events.	Problem-solvers who lack social awareness skills tend to have difficulty integrating feedback from a group of influencers. Consequently, the integration of group contributions into workable solutions may be retrained.
Relational skills refer to working with and engaging others in problem-solving endeavors.	Problem-solvers skilled at summarizing an influential group's diverse contributions take advantage of and factor most of the ideas into brainstorming options, selecting the best solution, and paving the way to a more informed implementation plan.	Limited relational skills among the group of influencers, particularly in a complex problem exchange, may be counterproductive and lead to disarray in the analysis and infusion of their diverse contributions into a problem-solving event.

As we consider the activation of the development process by crisis or motivational need, we want to ensure that we integrate the key role of *self* and *self-awareness* into these thoughts.

STONES OF REMEMBRANCE

The most valuable lesson learned from this chapter relates to the critical role of growth and development of those members of the community. This discussion elaborates on the development, drives, and resolution of life challenges using foundational research and thinking. As we approach a challenge, we are wise to assess the quality of the problem solver's developmental experiences and contributions to the developed self-dentity. What needs are met and managed with this challenge? How should this event be approached? Are the pre-decisions considered meeting the challenge for the individual or others? Erikson explains that an individual's free will allows for diverse options and possibilities in resolving each life-development crisis. Much like Bandura (1989) addresses individuals as agents of their actions and destinies, Erikson (1963) embraces the freedom and flow of individual development and self-identity. Life is changing, and the same is true regarding meeting and managing one challenge, which may have links to resolving the next lessons learned (see Table 3.2).

As you reflect on your personal development, remember that people can intentionally grow, adapt, and change to become better or not. The limits in initiating these changes are ours to identify, choose, and act upon as self-determined by investment and action.

CHAPTER 4

STRATEGY FOR ADDRESSING THE PROBLEM—BRAINSTORM AND REALITY-TEST

Our journey begins with an grocery cart analogy comparing it to raising a child. As the reader, you will act out this scenario written in the second person. "You arrive at your familiar grocery store and immediately look for a grocery cart. Conversely, your child is 5 years old and is accompanying you to the often-visited grocery store. Both events introduce a new life agenda. You, your child, and the basket cart begin an unfamiliar dance. You enter the store. Plan your path; you know exactly what you want. You tell yourself that this will be a quick shop-n-go experience. Your child has a different plan. Even with all the parenting books you have read, a surprising new challenge emerges. You direct your cart in one direction and quickly realize that the anticipated quick shop-n-go experience may not be as easy or quick as expected. While your child did not have wheels like the basket to direct the path, the child makes their needs known with much clarity." This example shows the individuality and uniqueness of each person's challenges even when they are participating in the same events.

This problem-solving conversation integrates research on development, social cognitive, and identity theories to focus on individual human development and its relationship to identity, change, and challenge. Conflict, as a challenge, allows for an expanded opportunity to be, learn, and grow. Bandura (2000) explains human agency, which is the capacity of

---

a person to act on and within a particular environment. An individual is born with a combination of self-defined biological features and genetically induced dispositions and unique personality traits that are environmentally influenced. Social cognitive-interactive relations is an example of a person's relationship with their environment and behavior. Bandura further explains that self-management develops with social and cognitive experiences. Bronfenbrenner's (1989, 1979) ecological systems theory contributes to this discussion, asserting that individuals and their environment constitute an integrated unit.

These research-based concepts influence the quality of a problem exchange and explain why every problem has a unique solution that is influenced by a problem solver's psychosocial, cognitive, and behavioral experiences. Erikson's (1959) crisis-motivated transitions describe life span in a different context. Erikson (1994) suggests that development is a series of transitions involving ongoing change and movement created to resolve life crises. Maslow (1998) contributes to this discussion by elaborating that personal motivations that address needs, including safety, security, and a sense of belonging, represent an investment in self-actualization.

The presented human development theories that inform the problem-solving processes consider (1) the intricate nature of human experiences, (2) the ongoing variations and perspectives in describing life development, and (3) the connection between the presented development and self-identity. Intersectionality can be illustrated by the layered tenets that people hold in their active developmental roles that motivate agency to address individual needs, values, and social settings, including interpersonal development within their social, cognitive, and biological parameters. Three questions emerge. Does human development influence the efficacy of problem management? Is problem-solving developmentally groomed? Is problem-solving development influenced? Referencing the chapter's opening story of the young child, the store offered an endless array of food, candy, and fun. The issue only surfaced when the parents' needs diverged from the baby's desires. Just as cognitive theory and social cognitive development can affect problem-solving, the goal is to explore the intersectionality of these theories when considering problem-solving effectiveness.

Jean Piaget's (1971) cognitive theory is crucial for understanding the complexity and significance of cognitive elements involved in change and problem-solving. Erikson (1963) approached the individual holistically and from a multicultural perspective. Piaget's cognitive theory comprises four stages that define a child's development and learning trajectory from childhood to adulthood. Stage 1: *Sensorimotor* makes an egocentric reference to the environment and its critical role in a child's learning, primarily through the senses and movement, and distinguishing that objects exist regardless of whether they are observable. The individual learns through senses and movement. Stage 2: *Pre-operational* is characterized by a focus on imaginative and pretend play but lacks flexibility in thought. For example, the girl must have one specific pair of shoes; no other pair will work. Stage 3: *Concrete Operational* entails increased literal and logical thinking, where the child is willing and able to consider the implications of thought. Stage 4: *Formal Operations* embodies abstract reasoning and the willingness to consider known and hypothetical features, such as philosophical, ethical, social, and political issues.

BRAINSTORMING

To solve a problem, one must identify the challenge within the problem, decide on potential courses of action, and select solutions that align with one's values. This brainstorming process fosters creative, divergent thinking, enabling reality testing and the opportunity to analyze, select feasible solutions, and consider the potential consequences of implementing these behavioral actions. All elements of the problem-solving process contribute to finalizing and developing a plan of action. Bandura's (1989, 2000) explanation of human agency and social cognitive interactive reciprocation, Bronfenbrenner's (1989) role of ecological systems on self and identity, Erikson's (1959) crisis-motivated transitions, Maslow's (1998) hierarchy of needs, and Piaget's cognitive (social and emotional) stages of development provide a diverse coalition of support for a problem-solving framework that aligns with the requisite social and emotional skills. Flavell (1971) suggests that Piaget's stages are more qualitative, with increasing stability found over time with social use. Thus, the human development discussion aims to assert that social and cognitive development support the acquisition of proficient problem-solving skills. In considering the road rage example, escalating the issue to get even with that driver creates a dysfunctional approach to problem-solving. What if a driver speeds up and gets in front to get even, and the driver pulls out a gun to shoot?

REALITY-TESTING

Once the brainstorming has concluded, it helps the analytical problem-solver develop a workable solution. Reality testing helps the problem-solver in further developing a workable solution. The time and investment in brainstorming each option aligns with a social cognitive triarchic interaction that involves the person, behavior, and environmental change. The question explored here addresses the implications of this option, along with the details involved when selected as part of the ultimate resolution plan. Returning to the road rage example, if, during the brainstorming stage, I decide after reality-testing that a better solution is to call the police. I pull over and call. I plan to implement a strategy for the solution. Obtain a description of the car and its license plate number. I assess the value of personal time and resource investment compared to the consequences of the required actions. Now is the time for a resolution plan, which outlines the implementation steps and activities. To illustrate how brainstorming and reality testing enhance the problem-solving process, we refer you to the LIBRE problem-solving model (Guerra, 2009a).

PROBLEM-SOLVING FRAMEWORK

The LIBRE problem-solving model (Guerra, 2016, 2015, 2009a) incorporates elements from social cognitive and goal-oriented theories to process a conflict-identified concern. Branded as LIBRE, the letters are acronyms for the problem-solving model actions. Collectively, LIBRE identifies the five steps of the problem-solving process: L-listen; I-identify the concern; B-brainstorm; R-reality-test; and E-encourage. The responses provide valuable insights into the problem-solving (PS) approach. This approach incorporates the PS's perspective on the challenging environment, the specifics of the problematic situation, and the individual's sense of agency, enabling the problem-solver (and, if included, the outside facilitator) to rely on self-awareness and self-management tools to complete the exchange.

In problem-solving, the parents of the young Mendoza man employed the Listen and List prompt and realized the dangers to their son, their family, and themselves. The political upheaval was devastating the people's morale. As they moved from the Identify the problem step, they immediately assessed the context of the problem. Now the question is, How do we safely bring our son home? The way the challenge manifests itself depends on the problem-solver's perception of its difficulty and significance. The LIBRE Model's advantage is that it provides space, a shared language, and a procedure for managing each step in the problem-solving process. It embodies ground rules, employs ethical and cultural competencies that acknowledge the vulnerability of the LIBRE process, and secures a sense of shared safety during and after using the LIBRE Model. These ground rules include:

- Respect—problem-solving within an esteemed cultural framework.
- Values and beliefs—representative of the problem-solvers' cultural, cognitive, social, and emotional "self."

- Safe—holds specific boundaries to define the exchange.
- Confidentiality/Defined learning—specific agreement of what the problem-solving steps are before beginning the activity (Guerra, 2016, 2009; Guerra et al., 2024).

The LIBRE Model provides an accessible and neutral space to reflect on their thoughts and emotions by deconstructing and analyzing the proposed unfiltered solution to the problem before evaluating the consequences. This example illustrates a young child's experiences with frequent "time-outs." Upon responding to the LIBRE Model prompts, he becomes most engaged in his brainstorming, explaining that he could "get a monkey to bite the coach so he could go out and play." As his facilitator reality-tested with him, he explained, "Once the coach knows that it is your monkey, you, me, and your monkey will be in time-out." "What else can you do so that you do not have to go into time-out?" The young problem-solver offered, "I can get a dog to bite the coach." Again, the facilitator explained that once the coach found out that the monkey and now the dog belonged to him, they also would be in time-out with him and the facilitator." Again, the facilitator asked, "What else could you do to avoid being in a time-out?" He paused and commented, "I know how not to go into time-out." The facilitator queried, "You do?" "Yes, all I have to do is sit down every time the coach tells me to, and I will avoid being in a time-out." The LIBRE Model plan prompted the problem-solver through to the E-encourage prompt. Now, the young kindergartner stated his plan: "Every time the coach tells me to sit down, I will." The following day, he returned to his facilitator to report that he had not been in time-out, "not even once." The problem-solving adjustment allowed the kindergartner to engage and empowered him to take actions that would help him meet his own goal.

The young child was able to name his challenge, brainstorm, and, with some assistance, reality-test his options before creating his best plan. Once he acted out his plan, he relaxed and enjoyed the self-earned success. A feeling of ownership is significantly important for future success in problem-solving. While the young child learned critical skills, brainstorming and reality-testing offered him a future strategy for self-managing conflict; success through applied learning exchanges provided confidence.

We return to the Mendoza family, presented in Chapter 1, to illustrate another example of an applied problem-solving event. The family had been living freely, operating their family business, which involved going into the surrounding towns to deliver bread and vegetables. The family was aware of the changing political climate; however, the Castillo mother, daughters, and Mendoza young men, along with their workers (who also served as bodyguards), continued to deliver groceries, and remained consistent in their visits to the neighboring towns. Each had their route, collected orders, and received money from those who purchased their products. One day, a young Mendoza brother, with the family's workers, happened to enter a small town where Pancho Villa and his men were actively recruiting. Promises of a "New Mexico," better conditions for all, and freedom from the oppressive political leaders of the day fueled the spirit of revolution. As the young Mendoza man listened, he was intrigued. Filled with love for the idea of adventure and the excitement of forging a new path, he told the family workers to return home and inform his parents that he would not be returning with them. The workers tried to dissuade him, but their words fell in dead ears, so they returned home and relayed the news to Augustina. She immediately notified her husband, Teodosio. Together, they collected copious notes and information, brainstormed and reality-tested many options before developing their plan. The identified challenge was straightforward; as far as they were concerned, they had to retrieve their son. Considering the limited time available, they had to prepare themselves for the potential challenges of securing a safe return. Brainstorming options, they began to reality-test what they should consider. They then developed their plan. The tools used to plan the strategy had elements from the plan development tools available when using the LIBRE Model. Teodosio would take the same men as before, with extra workers who would help as bodyguards as they entered the Pancho Villa camp. They would move quickly and quietly (see Table 4.1). Study this chart to help you through a problem-solving exercise to address a personal issue or challenge. We invite you to use it to chart out solutions to address your personal issue. Share with your family or friends and discuss how to improve or change the process.

Table 4.1

LIBRE Model Problem-Solving

LIBRE Model Prompt	Suggested Questions to Guide You Response to the LIBRE Model Prompt
Listen and List Challenges you are experiencing	Discomfort Cues Leading to a Problem 1. What is not working for you? 2. Identify events, conversations, behaviors, and other cues that define the feeling of discomfort. 3. What is going on in your "world" that is causing distress?

(Table continued on next page)

Table 4.1 (Continued)

LIBRE Model Prompt	Suggested Questions to Guide You Response to the LIBRE Model Prompt
Identify A Concern or Problem Related Question or Goal	*Pinpointing the Problem Through a Collaborative Approach* 1. Using the information gathered, what one problem emerges from an analysis of the discomfort cues? 2. Write out the identified problem as a question.
Brainstorm Unrealistic and realistic options, then prioritize	Writ out all possibilities to address the identified problem. 1. Make a list of those solutions consider quick solutions and those that will require more work. 2. To begin, prepare the proposed solutions for reality testing, order them by feasibility of implementation, labeling the first, second, and third. 3. Place an "X" by all remaining options that neither reflect you nor represent options you would never pursue.
Reality-test Consider implications, what it would look like as actionable behaviors	*Fitting the best solution to the problem-solver planning process* 1. Begin with the number one prioritized option and respond to the question "What would it look like if I acted on this option?" 2. Record your response, which may include contacting others for assistance or consultation. 3. Ask yourself this same question as you address each of the prioritized options (from the Brainstorm section).
Encourage Record Best Steps. Identify a Timeline for completing each step. Develop an implementation plan.	*Select a solution and plan for success; the level of involvement in planning and implementation will vary depending on the complexity of the problem and solution.* 1. Reflect on your work and the processing that you have completed. 2. Identify your best steps to your desired solution. Record each. 3. Opposite each action step, create a milestone. This may be in the form of a timeline with a list of resources or a date showing that the task has been completed. 4. You are formalizing your journey to success. You are holding yourself accountable only to yourself.

Mantra: (phrase or statement designed to anchor the problem-solver's investment in solving the identified problem) *I have the strength to create change!*

Once they found the young man, Teodosio approached him. The execution of the plan was a success. The young man approached his father, and everyone in the convoy returned home. Records show that the plan was a total success with a clock's precision.

Analysis of the problem-solving event. Problems are within or outside one's control. The family preserved the records for a closer study to investigate the incident. We recommend you study the process and context, how the family was able to mobilize so fast, and how the family galvanized the overwhelming support the family received during this crisis.

Young Mendoza left home early, as did the older brothers, mother, grandmother, and aunt, and all the volunteers. All returned home except young Mendoza. The challenge arose as the young son decided not to return home. The problem-solving dialogue has provided and offered the LIBRE Model analysis. In the **L** prompt, you **listen and list** to perceived and real problems amid contextual conditions. For example, you find out that a. the son is gone, b. the political climate, and c. need exists to act quickly. Recognizing the importance of their son's retrieval, the family was deeply concerned about his immediate safety. In the second prompt, **the I** you, with the person who has the problem, **identify** the focal concern as a question and define the stated and agreed-upon problem. An example of the question to use is: "How will we retrieve our son?" In the prompt, **B-brainstorming**, identify and consider both realistic and unrealistic options. An "X" was used to cross off non-feasible options. For example, select from these options: a. "question what happened," b. "hire someone to retrieve him," c. "let him go with Pancho Villa," d. "wait and see what happens," e. "retrieve him ourselves." After considering their generated solutions along with those eliminated, they select to focus on option e. "retrieve him themselves." The fourth prompt, **R-Reality-testing**, occurs as they begin to plan the key actions and consider the consequences of each. The fifth prompt, **E-encourage**, invites the problem-solver to develop a resolution plan with timelines.

THE LIBRE MODEL PROBLEM-SOLVING

Graphic Organizer

The problem-solving approach always includes the acronym L-listen and list, I-identify the problem, B-brainstorm, R-reality-test, and E-encourage prompts. However, an added feature is a graphic organizer to help problem-solvers with an illustrated picture of the problem-solving process (see Figure 4.1). The graphic outlines the five-step process: L-listen and list prompt found with the head of Figure 4.1, then moves to the I-identify a focal concern with the shoulders, then B-brainstorming and R-reality-testing with the midriff of the figure, and concluding with the two feet for the E-encourage response with the development of the resolution plan (Guerra, 2009a, 2015).

Figure 4.1

LIBRE Model Graphic Organizer

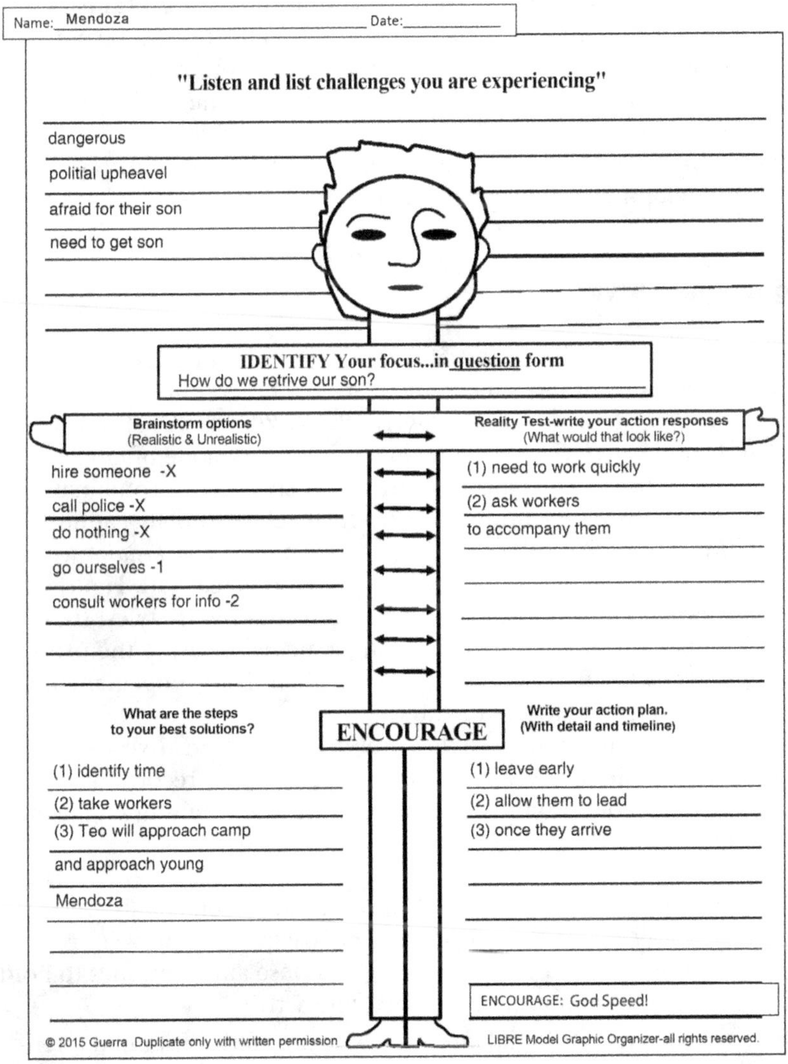
Name: Mendoza
Date:
"Listen and list challenges you are experiencing"
dangerous
politial upheavel
afraid for their son
need to get son
IDENTIFY Your focus...in question form
How do we retrive our son?
Brainstorm options
(Realistic & Unrealistic)
Reality Test-write your action responses
(What would that look like?)
hire someone -X
call police -X
do nothing -X
go ourselves -1
consult workers for info -2
(1) need to work quickly
(2) ask workers
to accompany them
What are the steps
to your best solutions?
ENCOURAGE
Write your action plan.
(With detail and timeline)
(1) identify time
(2) take workers
(3) Teo will approach camp
and approach young
Mendoza
(1) leave early
(2) allow them to lead
(3) once they arrive
ENCOURAGE: God Speed!
© 2015 Guerra Duplicate only with written permission
LIBRE Model Graphic Organizer-all rights reserved.

The graphic organizer has several advantages, (1) a recorded synthesis of the problem-solving process, (2) an anchoring visual to re-examine the developed plan executed; this allows the problem-solver(s) to consider what worked and what did not work, (3) an important data recording of attention provided during the execution of the problem-solving exchange, and (4) the identification of engagement styles (Guerra, 2009a). Two visual attentiveness patterns arise within the problem-solving exchange. They are: *Initial attention*—identified from the brainstorming and reality-testing data responses (Guerra, 2009b). The data reflects the problem-solvers' contextualized ecological setting, including brainstorming of workable and non-workable solutions and reality-testing responses to the question, "What will the option require behaviorally if acted upon?" Sustained attention—identified from the I-identify the problem and the E-encourage response data. The data reflects the problem-solver's specific commitment to the identified problem, the processing of the problem, and the development of an action plan.

Engagement Styles

Problems are within or outside one's control. Engagement drives success. Each of us has an engagement style. The graphic organizer aids in defining engagement styles (Guerra, 2007, 2009b, 2015) that we use to identify and categorize an individual's preferred mode of engagement in a problem-solving exchange. Engagement styles are a combination of two distinct levels of attention: *initial*, which refers to being attentive in responding to each problem-solving requirement, and *sustained*, which refers to holding full attention until a resolution is reached. Figure 4.3 is a graphic organizer defining each of the problem-solving styles. It defines how each one of us will address emerging issues while using the problem-solving process. While reviewing Figure 4.2, identify the engagement style associated with the behaviors in Table 4.2.

We use four engagement style combinations; a positive (+) and/or negative (-) problem-solver's response is visible and recorded for each of the LIBRE Model prompts (see Table 4.1). The resulting engagement styles are:

- (+) / (+) a positive initial and sustained attention equals an *actual engagement style*. This problem-solver is actively attentive in responding to each problem-solving response and continues to hold this full attention until the close of the activity.
- (-) / (+) a limited initial attention with a positive sustained attention equals a *goal-focused engagement style*.

- (+) / (-) a positive initial attention with a non-sustained attention equals a *venting engagement style*. This problem-solver is most interested in speaking about the problem, but interest lags when asked to speak to processing and /or creating a resolution to the problem. No resolution is created.
- (-) / (-) a non-attentive initial and sustained attention equals a *potential engagement style*. This person is guarded and/or *laissez-faire* about the processing of a problem. There is no interest in addressing any discussion of any problem. The completed LIBRE graphic organizer is almost blank with only repeated recordings of filtered words and thoughts (see Figure 4.2).

Figure 4.2

Problem-Solving Engagement Styles

Engagement Style: Potential

See self as a Skeptic or not wanting to invest.
- Failure to act promptly due to uncertainty.
- Filled with suspicion, hesitant to continue.
- Approaches recommendations and advice with caution and skepticism.

Engagement Style: Goal-Focused

Sees self as Decisive.
- Reacts instantly to solve problems.
- Makes informed decisions.
- Is accountable; does not procrastinate

Engagement Style: Venting

Sees self as a Procrastinator.
- Has a relentless pursuit of perfection while not wanting to commit.
- The possibility of decisions not working is troubling.
- Indecisiveness creates a crisis-maker.

(Figure continued on next page)

Figure 4.2 Continued

Engagement Style: Actual
Sees self as Compassionate.
• A listener who actively seeks input and values collaboration.
• Consistently respects and considers collaborators' advice.
• Shows empathy towards individuals dealing with problem-solving.

Table 4.2 provides the reader with the opportunity to review a set of behaviors related to the four problem-solving styles described in Figure 4.2. Write an X under the problem-solving styles that match the behavior. Once you have matched the behaviors to the problem-solving style, draw a circle around the X that matches those behaviors that describe you.

Once you have circled the behaviors that define you, select the problem-solving style with the most circled Xs. This self-select assessment has limitations, but overall, it provides a sense of direction and inclination towards a predominant style.

Table 4.2

An Activity to Match Behaviors and Problem-Styles

Behavior	Problem-Solving Styles			
	Potential	Goal Focus	Venting	Actual
Makes informed decisions				
Suspicious and hesitant to act				
The possibility of decisions not working is troubling.				
Filled with suspicion, hesitant to continue.				
Is accountable; does not procrastinate.				
Has a relentless pursuit of perfection while not wanting to commit.				
Approaches recommendations and advice with caution and doubt				

(Table continued on next page)

Table 4.2 Continued

Behavior	Problem-Solving Styles			
	Potential	Goal Focus	Venting	Actual
Indecisiveness creates a crisis-maker.				
Consistently respects and considers collaborators' advice.				
A listener who actively seeks input and values collaboration.				
Shows empathy towards individuals dealing with problem-solving.				
Failure to act promptly due to uncertainty.				

Mendoza Engagement Style

The Mendoza parents knew their son was empathetic, benevolent, trustworthy, and caring; his parents made sure that their children received a good education and had taught them to be the best they could be. They also prepared them to deal with the potential dangers in their unfamiliar environment. They used a goal-focused engagement style to plan the retrieval of their young son. Table 4.2 depicts the initial and sustained attention to address the challenge the family was facing, including assessment of options and the development processing options, and development of the Mendoza Parents' Plan.

The Mendoza Parents' Plan provides minimal initial information, other than the dangers of delaying action; information shared only focused on their son and his return. The key for us is the style and approach taken. The goal-focused plan was deliberate, and the outcome data collected shows fidelity in its implementation.

STONES OF REMEMBRANCE

We must carefully consider several things before bringing this chapter to a close. The discussion on human experience and development was complex, offering us much to consider. The conversation about problem-solving urges us to examine the everyday community from different perspectives.

While we may all experience the same event, we will see it differently. Each person takes part as a separate agent with distinct experiences. As such, we must address a situation where shifting *engagement style* considerations have community implications (see Table 4.2).

This topic is a precursor to future chapters that will cover the fundamentals of problem-solving. As we close, several takeaways are clear:

1. Personal growth and development—We want to attend to self and identity. As there are seasons in life, there is change. Change and investing in change begin with the self.
2. Conflict and challenge are inevitable. We will encounter unwelcome change and conflict. Therefore, we must invest in self-development that focuses on a healthy identity, self-awareness, social awareness, self-management, and self-actualization.
3. Problem-solving is a life skill. To emphasize the importance of self-development, our goal is to invest in becoming a well-balanced and skilled group of individuals ready to face challenges. Our workforce must become proficient in problem-solving, which will soon be a required skill.
4. Support and encouragement from those who are close and valued accelerate growth.

This chapter invites you to review and explore your observations about the value of the theoretical model. When confronted with obstacles, remember the skills you have gained, your temperament, and the unique contributions you will make to your community and the people you meet. An opportunity to explore change and what that might involve exists.

CHAPTER 5

REFLECTIONS ON PROBLEM-SOLVING

Our journey now leads us to consider problem-solving as self-care, growth, and wellness investment. Incorporating the "best of who we are" in problem-solving does not occur automatically. Essential skills to cultivate involve self-growth, self-awareness, self-reflection, and self-monitoring. For example, ongoing self-growth encompasses self-reflection and growth as an intentional and aspirational pursuit.

Investing in the person's best self becomes a criterion and a critical advantage as we approach people and negotiate unfamiliar spaces. You are now more attentive to your thinking, feelings, and psychosocial willingness to engage, leading to more focused attention on your further growth and development. The question of managing change becomes a challenge that could disrupt relationships with family, friends, and associates. The problem-solver must be prepared to address this issue of damaged relationships. Embracing self-reflection and change also propels you forward to new and more effective communication methods. A natural extension of becoming a wise problem-solver is the evolution of self-identity. We are now investing in listening rather than critiquing on demand. I recently visited an elderly friend, and as we chatted, she whispered in my ear, "It's hard being 98." I hugged her and assured her that she was doing an excellent job. Admittedly, I know nothing of her daily demands or what it is like to be her age, but I can listen, hear, and appreciate her shared wisdom with encouragement. Change is our constant companion, and like age, it presents an opportunity for us to grow into our best selves. We begin with a discussion on investment.

From Problem-Solving to Responsible Decision-Making,
pp. 53–63
www.emeraldgrouppublishing.com

Problem-solving approaches often mirror individual development. There are lessons to be learned from the decisions and mistakes made. Let us engage the young Mendoza family at this point. The emotional reaction they experienced when informed by their workers that their son had decided to join Pancho Villa must have been a significant blow, creating a wave of emotion, panic, and urgency. It was a call for all the family, siblings, and grandparents to become involved. The parents loved all their children, but at this moment, their entire attention and investment were focused on this one son, allowing them to move quickly and retrieve him. The other consideration was their son's willingness and decision to hear and respond to his father's request to return home.

Willingness to Grow. We rarely consider the decision to grow or postpone our growth. Growth and change never stop, occurring daily. Reflecting on my visit with a friend, our conversation centered on her courage, faith, and fortitude. She had come a long distance to attend the funeral of her nephew. She was sad, but at peace with his passing. Without speaking directly about any specific life themes, she communicated volumes in grace in how she handled herself, and her personal life decisions, life development, and challenges. In that moment, I noticed her self-awareness and willingness to articulate her associated age accommodations. Bandura's (2000) concept of agency describes each of us as responsible selves with affirmations for a motivated life, promoting maximum participation in all. We each have a life, and our actions in life make a difference. We are not passively wandering on this life journey with steps outside our control; our steps are ours to take or not. We determine our response to growth challenges in our willingness to revisit, reflect, and change in an intentional direction that better represents our true evolving self-identity. Aging and our physical development regulate the changes that occur. These individualized life investments offer direction and present an opportunity.

Creating Your Whole Person's Self-in-Identity. The invitation is here to "lean into and breathe," to make time to revisit earlier stages of development, to resolve negative inclinations, to invest in you, the whole person, to integrate the assets, skills, and opportunities that you have been afforded, and to make your objective to be your *best-self* now. Be keenly aware of the time investment and most aware of when to invest or not. You must invest in yourself to live the *best life*. The first step involves defining criteria. Values may be one consideration, along with role models that have given insights to move forward into those best-self spaces. Developmental theories can provide valuable insights to initiate this introspective journey. The more we learn about ourselves, the better we will become at honing personal assets to adjust, modify, and grow. Extending skills in self-investment will provide a foundation for how we approach problem-solving and future life-changing events.

Self-Care in Development. We begin this section with caution; self-investment and exploration may lead to being perceived as selfish or self-centered, but this is not necessarily true. Self-investment contributes to social exchange efficacy. A lack of self-investment may contribute to distortions in one's perception of self and others. Recalling Maslow's (1998) hierarchy of needs, we are social, cognitive, and emotional beings with people skills to personalize the problem-solving process. For instance, people become more self-aware of how they present themselves upon entering a room. Usually, these people pay attention to how others respond to them. Social awareness is critical in a person's ability to manage positively and minimize future negative exchanges. We are fortunate to have a wealth of research to draw upon in addressing the self.

PRINCIPLES OF A WHOLE PERSON

Carl Rogers (1962). Maslow (1998) and Kaufman (2000) provide content for the tenets of this next section. Our directional movement from problem-solvers to responsible decision-makers emphasizes personal, whole-person self-development as a foundation for problem-solving skills. While it is not easy to go back to an earlier pain-associated time for self-reflection, it can be a lost lesson if the revisit does not occur. Imagine a time when someone betrayed you; reframe that earlier memory to consider what was learned from that experience. A tendency to be suspicious and unwilling to trust anyone remained. Since that early memory, much has changed, rendering that mistrusting inclination a non-functional orientation. Yes, you learned a valuable lesson; you also learned that not everyone is trustworthy. You may have also defined what trust means to you and who is a trustworthy and dependable person. More importantly, you revisit the concept of trust and its application to oneself and others. Reciprocal self-reflection helps one see the value of trust, but more importantly, it enables one to see oneself as a trusting person who distinguishes between trust and mistrust. This journey leads to a deeper understanding and appreciation of oneself as a whole person. In self-exploration toward redefining self as a "whole person." Self-exploration helps in redefining oneself as a "whole person." The following seven principles provide additional considerations in defining the whole person (Kaufman, 2000).

Principle 1: Accept Your Whole Self, Not Just Your Best Self. Carl Rogers (1972) is most noted for his work in cultivating the true, authentic whole self. Using this definition, the examination of the whole self leads us to consider all aspects of who we are, not just one part of ourselves. For example, the *self* embraces the "good hair days," the "unmanageable hair days, "and all the days in between. While this explanation is a light example, the intention is to see ourselves as others do and to offer esteem. It is easy to appreciate ourselves when those around us model and define us using positive descriptors. This type of interaction suggests social acceptance and admiration. When appreciation of a "good hair day" is valued, the same appreciation for the person should also be provided on a "bad hair day." What happens when we stumble on ourselves and even offend with a "bad hair day" comment? If we are self-aware, we reflect on and minimize negative consequences; when we fumble, we apologize and accept that this, too, is part of who we are. Kaufman (2000) adds to the discussion by asking, "Which potentialities within me do I wish most to spend my limited time cultivating, developing, and actualizing in this world." The gains will be made in those areas. According to Maslow (1998), his hierarchical approach to self-actualization can also prompt us to ask ourselves, "What needs or areas are you willing to address that will allow you to be a self-actualized, whole person truly?" All good definitions that encourage us to accept our whole self and recognize that it is a process that should help us along this life journey. We can find the answer to self-security in identity in the definition. Kaufman (2000) suggests that securing a safe and encouraging environment is important for beginning to explore the acceptance of oneself, with a caveat labeled "authenticity positivity bias," defined as the tendency always to find it easier to accept those aspects of oneself that are pleasing to oneself and others. This one-dimensional view of self is that to become a whole self, you need to embrace the "bad hair days," features that are not appealing, such as a quick temper or judgmental inclinations. As we embrace and value our entire selves, we can then see the value in both selfishness and altruism.

Principle 2: Learn To Trust Your Self-Actualizing Tendency. As we explore who we are, we also need to revisit Erikson's (1959) early stages of development. For example, trust versus mistrust takes a fresh look at that stage of development, but this time from the perspective of a whole self (or an invested person searching for wholeness). Now, we do not depend on others to meet our needs; we assume responsibility for meeting them ourselves. Authentically love self-actualized tendencies, whether they are selfish or altruistic, and then embrace and trust oneself to respond in a manner that best represents the affected person. We can now examine my acculturation, embracing what we value and moving away from those areas that do not reflect the "best self," the self we aspire to become. Embracing self-identity, we are not victims; we consider ourselves a whole person, an agent responsible for our actions. Maslow's (1943) articulation of needs introduces self-growth openings to explore, become, and be. The "how" begins with a safe and secure space that you create in the care of yourself.

Principle 3: Become Aware of Your Inner Conflicts. As we explore, tendencies emerge that do not align with the person we believe ourselves to be, introducing inner conflicts. The lesson here is that even as change and conflict occur all around us, conflict also occurs within our deepest selves. Maslow (1943) viewed this as part of the motivated drive to meet needs, stating, "Man is a wanting animal." Rather than reacting to the idea of experiencing inner conflict, Kaufman (2000) suggests that we should consider the message being communicated. For example, as we consider Maslow's (1998) hierarchy of needs, each need also represents a conflict. I am hungry. I need to eat. The conflict arises from deciding when to eat, what to eat, and how much to eat. The inner discourse continues until decisions are made and needs are met. The more aware we become of our inner conflicts, the more we have a renewed potential to be better. The awareness enables better decision-making regarding inner conflicts.

Principle 4: Look Out for Lopsided Development. Our developmental journey toward becoming a whole person is marked by the harsh reality that development is lopsided. Development is not even smooth. Consider the observant gifted child. As the child cognitively develops and increases in skills much more quickly than his peers, social skills often fall behind, thereby creating challenges. If we pause to consider why this might occur, we can understand that differences in ability, preferences, and experiences play a role in problem-solving. The child's investment is reinforced as he does what he is good at doing and enjoys doing. Invest in external self-reinforcement for a greater return on investment. As people seeking wholeness, we want to be gentle with ourselves, and we may not have development at the top of our game plans. Self-awareness helps us address the developmental areas that may need revisiting. As a whole person addresses areas of growth, growth can occur. Erikson (1959) saw these gains as examples of human growth and development.

Principle 5: Create the Best Version of Yourself. Invest in "self" to move to wholeness. Self-awareness is encouraging because it frees us to define what the "best version" of ourselves is. Looking into that mirror at what is and what can be is grounding. We can affirm our values, assets, and experiences and, along with the foundational tenets, anchor us so that we can begin to explore what more there is to be learned. What additional skills can be developed to create a better version of "self?" "What" and "how" become important considerations in examining personal change and development. Anchoring strengths are important; it offers a link to the security of the past, allowing us to explore the present and future. Values become a weight to hold us securely as we consider all other changes. Be gentle in learning and managing safe environments; change can be disorienting.

Principle 6: Strive for Growth, not Happiness. *Growth* and *happiness* are not the same. This principle embodies a value that prioritizes personal growth over the pursuit of *happiness*. Consider this principle carefully and be available to determine if the investment is to "strive for *growth*, not *happiness*." As we consider wholeness, *growth* becomes a value. For many people, *growth* is more important and should not be compromised to achieve *happiness*. If we have but one life in our quest for wholeness, we should not reduce life to a counterintuitive one-dimensional investment. Our quest may be to consider the integration of growth and happiness. Wholeness in *growth* and *happiness* should complement one another. Would I want to outgrow my community and end up alone? These are decisions to ponder.

Principle 7: Harness the Power of Your Dark Side. This principle supports examining *growth* and *happiness* together. For example, my personal growth commitment is to become a significantly more skilled person in my craft. However, I may also be releasing darkness to those closest to me. Why? My self-oriented advancements will not be based on the "old ways." Therefore, I will need to dedicate the time and energy required to reflect on myself and regain the skillful footing to move forward. This self-oriented investment looks selfish.

There is no room for anyone else because I only have time to address my needs: physiological, safety and security, love and belonging, and self-esteem in my quest to be self-actualized. This was not what Maslow (1943) intended as a step toward self-actualization. Self-awareness is a significant step in management. The lopsided developmental pathways we knowingly or unknowingly follow hold power and impact. What we engage in and how we engage are as much a matter of good and dark consideration. Each state of mind is found within who we are as whole people and the invested decisions we make.

ENGAGEMENT IN PROBLEM-SOLVING

As a whole person, we have considered principles and elements to guide us as we engage in the problem-solving process. We determine our investment in each challenge encountered. Unfortunately, if we do not intentionally attend, we may find ourselves stepping into challenges and resolutions as passive participants rather than active ones due to a lack of attentiveness. Self-awareness and growth are essential for self-managed and self-groomed problem-solving (Guerra, 2016). Extending this self-actualized whole-person in problem-solving, four engagement styles can be taken on to consider a problem and context and to adjust your participatory role. To examine each engagement style, let us consider the Mendoza family as an example of each:

Potential Engagement

This investment is minimal and guarded (Guerra, 2009b). The problem-solver is not completely withholding self-investment but appears uninterested in assuming an observer role. Take young Mendoza, who has now joined Pancho Villa's men. He is unfamiliar with foreign social exchanges that have an impact on his identity development and personal investment. He wonders if he has joined too quickly without considering the consequences. When a challenge is presented, "What are we going to do for food? Where can we get some?" He says nothing. While he, too, is hungry and knows where to find food, he offers nothing in return for a problem-solving exchange. He shrugs his shoulders with a lack of interest.

Venting Engagement

This investment is intended to provide problem details rather than a solution. Unique and distinct from potential engagement, this person initially invests but fails to sustain the investment to identify a solution (Guerra, 2009). Young Mendoza makes daily runs into the neighboring cities. He vents, telling the workers that his older brothers always have the advantage and privilege of selecting the towns along their routes. He can never go to the big cities. He does not have the seniority, nor will he ever, so as he continues to be sent into his small town, he vents. "Nothing ever presents adventure or fun along this path; every day, I do the same thing. I go to the same small towns closest to home, drop off the bread at the same bakeries and vegetables at the same markets, pick up the money, and return home." "I don't ever get to go into the big cities, because my older brothers have already selected them." The problem he identified was the need for adventure. In venting during problem-solving, he feels and sees himself as helpless (Guerra, 2006). He never considers the possibility of negotiating a solution, nor is he willing to invest time in the negotiation process.

Goal-Focused Engagement

A goal-focused engagement style is the opposite of venting. While venting engagement is characterized as an initial investment that is not sustained, the goal-focused problem-solving investment holds all attention in reserve until the problem is identified and addressed. Currently, the problem-solver is becoming the most invested. The focus and attention are on sustaining the investment and identifying a solution.

There is little to no initial investment in the context of the problem (Guerra, 2009b). Augustina Mendoza was involved in this goal-focused engagement. Once she was informed of her son's decision to join Pancho Villa, her problem-solving investment failed to consider how her son felt or what contributed to triggering his decision, nor was she interested in what her other sons or family thought about her son's decision to join Pancho Villa, instead her immediate problem-solving focus was to contact her husband. She was keenly aware that, as a woman in the early 1900s, she could not retrieve her son herself; she needed to contact her husband to resolve the issue of bringing her son home. This single-focused problem-solving approach included a plan with detailed actions to free and bring her husband home. He would then be able to retrieve their son.

Actual Engagement

The actual engaged problem-solver is self-aware, reflective, and attentive to details, exhibiting investment throughout the entire problem-solving process. The problem-solver is initially invested in the surroundings associated with the challenging event. As the challenging event unfolds, the problem-solver embraces the complexity of attending to those contextually involved and the potential impact as resolutions are considered. The problem-solver is actively involved; initial and sustained attention in brainstorming and reality-testing options can be observed before developing a detailed plan (Guerra, 2009b). Teodosio Mendoza exemplifies this investment style. His workers come to him with the instructions provided by his wife. Likely, Teodosio asks many questions as he returns home. They included: "Is his wife safe? Where are the other sons? How long ago did this occur?" His initial attention is drawn to the context and sustained attention to the presented problem resolution.

Meanwhile, more contextual questions are asked about the event, "Did the workers try to talk the young Mendoza into returning home?" "What are options that should be considered as they begin developing a plan?" As he returns home, he considers, "Who should he take to retrieve his son?" Together, Teodosio and his wife created the plan; he and his workers successfully implemented it, and young Mendoza safely returned home.

ENGAGEMENT STYLE IN A SELF-ACTUALIZED PERSON

Assuming that engagement styles are noteworthy and advantageous, any focus on their implications for problem-solving cannot be ignored (Guerra, 2016). The engagement styles are learned, and with self-awareness, can be effective (Guerra, 2015). Introducing the whole person as a self-actualized individual allows us to appreciate the value of problem-solving engagement style selection. Not all problems are best addressed in one manner. Extending this concept to a simple analogy, different tools are needed for different jobs. Sometimes, a hammer; other times, a screwdriver is the better choice. Ongoing research on engagement styles has found that individuals have engagement style preferences, whether they are aware of them or not (Guerra, 2022, 2016, 2015). Self-awareness and management, as key elements of self-actualization (Maslow, 1998), are essential in determining problem-solving engagement styles in response to a problem's specific needs (Guerra, 2015).

For the self-actualized person, engagement considerations include the challenge and assessing the seriousness of the problem. The initial investment involves listening to self and considering one's well-being and awareness, even as brainstorming and reality-testing are being considered. The sustained investment introduces the implications of continued attention in addressing the problem and the willingness to live with the outcome, impact, and consequences of the solution. As with all problem solvers, normal cognitive capacity is required. Engagement investment usage will vary similarly with age, awareness, and experience. It is ideal to consider preferred engagement styles about a problem. If I am hungry and need to eat, a goal-focused approach is likely to meet my needs best. If I am preparing for a new job, an actual engagement might be a better match. Let us examine the investment, self-awareness, and management considerations of each engagement style this time as a self-actualized person who is both self-aware, regulated, selfish, and altruistic. What is their impact on the feasibility, affordability, and potential success of a solution?

Potential Engagement (-/-)

A self-actualized potential person is aware of their limited or filtered investment. The person enters the PS experience the full awareness that there will be no sustained investment and they see this as an asset to the effective problem-solver. Investment refers to the ability to achieve intentional social impact in solutions created to address a problem or issue. If a self-discussion reveals an intention to limit investment, solutions may fail to show any benefit to the actors affected in a problem-solving event. A self-discussion that ignores investing may hurt intricately links to the pivotal self-actualized point that Maslow (1943) describes as the awareness of both selfish and selfless, altruistic beings. The individual may trust that the process will resolve itself; thus, there is no overt need to engage in problem-solving or invest. The potential participation in this case is positive. The reverse is also a possibility; the individual may select to remove self from the problem-solving, creating further injury. The individual may assume it is better not to invest, even if injury to the self is a consequence. This approach is a negative consequence of the potential engagement. Developmentally, the younger PSs will need more guidance. If the individual is aversive to conflict, the PS may prefer this potential engagement style.

Venting Engagement (+/-)

A positive aspect of venting is that it allows all expressions to be shared without requiring an investment in change. Maslow (1968) recognized that not all needs are always met by self-actualized people, for example, a person on a diet who is hungry. The development continues at the same time as hunger prevails, creating distortion and increased attention to food. The negative impact of venting when hunger exists is that the need is identified, but the problem-solver is not invested in meeting the identified need; there is no sustained effort to develop a solution. The actualized person identifies the problem but does not invest in the solution; may see no value in this investment. If needs are not met when, developmentally, why invest the energy? A young child vents and cries to get needs met, but stops when no one is present.

Goal-Focused Engagement (-/+)

A benefit of being goal-focused is that the individual decides to invest in the problem, is attentive to it, and takes guaranteed action. Augustina had the singular goal of bringing her husband home so that he could address the problem concerning their son. The negative is that being goal-focused, the solution is the critical feature, and all other considerations are minimized. The goal may be met, but "Power of Your Dark Side"/Principle 7 may have created havoc in meeting the goal. For example, "being run over by a black Friday Shopper." Developmentally, goal-oriented engagement, like the other styles, is learned and managed to meet personal needs. Adolescents and adults who recognize the advantages of this straight-forward engagement style may intentionally focus their energies on the solution-oriented approach.

Actual Engagement (+/+)

The positive aspect of the engaged style is the contemplative, reflective thoughtfulness that is assumed throughout the entire problem-solving exchange. The problem-solver is initially invested from the beginning to the close of the event, offering all their experience, skills, and wisdom to seek the best resolution for all involved. A drawback to the engaged problem-solver is the intricacy of problem-solving, which can require more time and slow down the resolution process. Developmentally, this approach is not often practiced by young children; they lack life experience and problem-solving skills. Thus, as adolescents and adults mature, greater awareness and skill development are possible in considering problems from multiple perspectives, both concrete and abstract. Bandura's (2006) agency presents a summarizing thought, explaining that no one is a bystander in their life; there is engagement in all behavior. The advantage of self-actualized problem-solver is the visibility of investment (Guerra, 2015). Mantra: *Things may be what they are, but I will select how I will invest.*

STONES OF REMEMBRANCE

As we close this chapter, we emphasize the importance of becoming a whole person, caring for oneself, investing, and becoming effective problem-solvers. In development and growth, our timeline is ours to manage. How we invest and decide our priorities is a moment to celebrate. We are social beings, composed of the complexity of who we each are as individuals and as members of our communities. Wonderful in potential, goal orientation, and intentionality. Awareness of self, feelings, thinking, and being drives us to profound thought and expanded use of our skills.

SECTION II

RESPONSIBLE DECISION-MAKING

CHAPTER 6

THE STORY CONTINUED

An immediate response to the growing challenges was the available opportunities for their family and business to succeed. What are the opportunities? Do they qualify for those jobs? What are the work requirements? These questions were factored and considered using a problem-solving strategy. To answer the fundamental and most important question became the challenge. Do we go or stay in Mexico? The family discussed, listened to, and considered all potential challenges within their environmental context. Other concerns related to this foundational question included, Should they wait and see how things unfold, or should they begin making plans?

What would be the outcome of losing all that they had created? In the event they decided to stay, What would be involved? If the plans were to leave, What would that include? Would they leave together? If some family members went first, Who would remain behind, and for how long? They were not seeking a short-term solution; instead, they were considering changes to their family and business life. They must consider all available options.

Fortunately, in 1912, Teodosio received his alien work permit, also known as a green card. Wanting to give his family options for a better life, he came to Texas and worked for the Watson family as an indentured servant, learning about Texas life. While working in Texas, he used his mastered farming skills. His wife and family kept him informed of Mexico's political climate while he continued to travel back and forth. Meanwhile, in Texas, Mr. Watson offered to help him with a transition to Texas if that

From Problem-Solving to Responsible Decision-Making,
pp. 67–70
www.emeraldgrouppublishing.com

was his decision. He also volunteered to help Teodosio by informing him about the property laws governing the purchase of land by a foreigner and encouraging him to invest in land that would provide his 11 sons with opportunities to work the land.

Through a strong work ethic and the expansion of their business, the Castillo-Mendoza family gained wealth and lived comfortably. The family and their mercantile business grew. Meanwhile, they remained keenly aware of the 1910 upheaval in their city, state, and nation. As citizens, they relied on governmental reports to learn about Mexico's precarious environmental and economic conditions. Concerned about the economic and social upheavals, the Castillo and Mendoza families devoted considerable time to listening and engaging with workers, the community, business partners, and associates.

Their 1913 reality involved continued work despite economic instability and the fact that they were living in a country that was no longer safe. Reports revealed that rebels and patriots were going from town to town, killing, raping, and taking the men to join their armies. The Mendoza family, while preserving the integrity of their business, reflected on the stream of information they had received. Augustina and Teodosio, with their eleven sons and one daughter, felt vulnerable after having experienced a close encounter in retrieving their 16-year-old son, who had innocently ventured out. While they were grateful for his quick recovery, they were concerned and felt wary about their son's thinking and future. The underlying thought was the challenge they now faced with their son and the safety of the entire family. They might not be as fortunate the next time as they had been with the son who veered and landed with Pancho Villa. The thoughtful Mendoza parents learned the importance of maintaining a watchful oversight of the needs and wants of all their children.

Teodosio returned to his wife and family and was present when their son met Pancho Villa. This interaction only heightened their need to consider change. The importance of family participation in the decision-making process became a key consideration in the final decision to move. Teodosio and Augustina revisited their values and commitments. They affirmed that family was the most important value, and their commitment was to their family business. The family's safety and increasing political and business risks constituted a significant concern. From oral history and family documents, the Mendoza and Castillo families examined the problem using the same contextual elements of the day, but this time with a larger, responsible decision-making approach that included collaboration with their family. This problem-solving event was complex; they were intent on considering their livelihoods, business impacts, asset management, and well-being. Their shared listening exchange led the two families apart from one another. The Mendoza family decided that their problem would be to focus on moving to Texas. Augustina had lived in Mexico since birth. So had the entire family lived in Mexico all their lives. While political challenges were occurring in Mexico, Texas faced its own challenges.

Texas Rangers were moving freely across the state. Moreover, they randomly killed Mexicans. They would not guarantee their safety, therefore, how to address the risks became another problem. Finding a safe place to move became their next challenge. Staying in Mexico was not an option; too many risks with the unstable government and harsh conditions in every city scared them. Furthermore, the political instability would negatively affect their mercantile business. After considering the options, the Castillos discovered that significant problems and issues existed that required their immediate attention.

Originally from Spain, the Castillos were now considering a return to their homeland. Their pressing need was to decide when and where to live. They deliberated the invitation to move to Texas, but to them, this was another foreign country. They listened to the proposed invitation but decided to return to Spain, their country of origin. The Castillo parents decided to leave their property to their daughter, Augustina, and her family. Adapting to a different culture was challenging, and the complexity of a new life in a foreign country, along with its consequences, shifted their focus back to their country of origin. The Castillos struggled through the problem-solving approach and created their departure plans.

The family extensively used the responsible decision-making approach to assist with the considerable number of complex problems and issues associated with their relocation to Texas. Complex problems ranged from adjusting to an unfamiliar environment, making new friends, building homes, starting careers supported by experience and guided learning, and setting goals for a better life. One of the older sons became engaged, posing a new challenge to the newly arrived family. Teodosio and his newly engaged son worked as a team and created a separate agreement that when the time to marry arrived, Teodosio would accompany his son to the wedding. The married couple would also bring the bride's mother to join them in Texas. What a deal!

Records indicate that Mendoza and other extended family members moved to Texas in 1913. As promised, the family-built *casas* (homes) on the purchased land for the Mendoza family and their extended family. Augustina and Teodosio hired someone to continue to run the original Mexico business. The entire Mendoza family and extended family moved to Texas in 1913. The one-engaged son accompanied the family. As agreed, in 1914, Teodosio and his son returned to Mexico. His son and his bride married in the church, and they (bride, mother-in-law, and Mendoza men) then took a train back to Texas. The day began with an early morning marriage, followed by a train ride to Texas. When they arrived, the entire family was there to greet them; reunited, they began their lives in Texas.

The Mendoza family carried their commitment to their faith, family, and work values. However, this time, it was the second-generation young Mendoza men and women who pursued their chosen careers, despite Teodosio's large landholdings and operating the original family bakery. Neither business survived as a livelihood for the family.

Each of the Mendoza offspring created new life pathways. The land was divided equally among the 12 children, and they were free to do as they wished with their inherited property.

STONES OF REMEMBRANCE

Challenges are an inevitable part of life. People and things change unexpectedly. Self-awareness can help in self-management and with learning. Modeled within this story was their sustained attention to remain open to listening and learning. It became a discerning advantage for them as a family. Skilled social interactions with others beyond their immediate network also had significant impacts. Such was the interaction with the Watsons, who mentored and provided key information to the Mendoza family. The openness to listen, trust, and be self-aware helped all involved, individually and collectively, in navigating this new beginning.

CHAPTER 7

CONTEXT AND RELATIONAL CLIMATE— COLLABORATIVE LISTENING

COLLABORATIVE LISTENING

Transforming problem-solving into responsible decision-making events requires a revisit of definitions. The primary distinction between a straightforward problem-solving process and an accountable decision-making method lies in the complexity of the problem and the number of people involved in the decision-making process. Problem-solving is a direct, planned exchange. For example, begin by identifying a problem that is within your control, process it, explore and generate brainstorming options before employing reality-testing criteria to scrutinize and select one from a list of potential solutions. After thoughtful consideration of the identified problem and feasible solutions, develop a resolution plan with timelines to benchmark and evaluate the outcome.

Responsible decision-making involves a similar intentional problem-solving process; however, the involvement of multiple people in assessing potential solutions and the complexity of managing the process intensify the collaborative nature of the activity, making the outcome an informed decision. For example, responsible decision-making involves collective consensus-building across each step of problem-solving (L-I-B-R-E). The process calls for diverse participants representing multiple perspectives, regardless of their engagement styles and development stage. Thus, the

From Problem-Solving to Responsible Decision-Making,
pp. 71–79
www.emeraldgrouppublishing.com

facilitator manages and leads the process. Undoubtedly, the actual engage-ment style is a strong fit for supporting and sustaining the processing of complex challenges (Guerra, 2016; Guerra & Carrillo-Bollinger, 2011). For example, the Mendoza and Castillo families met to identify their problems.

The original problem-solving team now became two separate teams identifying problems and issues unique to each family's life efforts. The Castillo family identified their problem as "What preparations do we need to make to return to Spain?" For the Mendozas, once the concern surfaced, the issue was, "When is the plan to move to Texas?" Finding the problem or issue did not require too much discussion; the questions were direct. The problem-solver jumped into the brainstorming and reality-testing steps. After intense divergent and convergent deliberations, the families settled and prioritized the distinct options, assessing each option for feasibility and affordability. Problem-solvers developed a shared resolution plan with timelines and benchmarks to evaluate the plan and its outcome.

Responsible decision-making (RDM) is a collaborative and facilitated process of problem-solving conducted within the community. Significant distinctions exist between the RDM approach and the single problem-solver approach in the imbedded substructures and the number of people involved in the decision-making process. For instance, rather than one person (or family) deciding on a specific problem, both the Castillo and Mendoza families came together to address the problem as a unified team. In contrast, when Teodosio and Augustina, as parents, became aware of their son's decision, they immediately made a single-viewpoint problem-solving decision to retrieve their son from Pancho Villa. The parents did not seek input from young Mendoza or their other family members. They solely approached the problem, defined it, processed it, and resolved it. This direct approach views the problem only from the position of the prob-lem-solver(s); only this person(s) manages and resolves the challenge.

The inclusive and responsible decision-making (RDM) collaborative approach focuses on community, at times inviting one of the problem solvers to assume a lead role (facilitator) to help guide the problem-solving community. RDM is "the ability to make caring and constructive choices about personal behavior and social interaction across diverse situations" (CASEL, 2003). The RDM approach includes all participants involved in the consequences of the plan. Consider the engagement styles, develop-mental experiences, and identity self-awareness as powerful and influential elements of active members as they identify the problem, process it, and consider the potential of each proposed resolution. The ideal facilitator welcomes all affected actors or parties to contribute to the RDM process and embodies the qualities associated with the *actual engagement* style. This engagement style is known for sustaining the integration of multiple opinions and will not rush the group to a resolution too quickly. The facilitator has the responsibility of encouraging and supporting honesty, frankness, and sincerity to consider diverse thoughts while guiding the complex challenge process (Guerra, 2016; Guerra & Carrillo-Bollinger, 2011). Prominent distinctions between the two approaches involve processing time, participant involvement, complexity, and the degree of inclusion in the problem-solving process.

The entire RDM event integrates the values of community, participant development, engagement styles, and respectful, active listening (to each other) to address a complex need with far-reaching implications (Guerra & Carrillo-Bollinger, 2011). The self-actualized person (Kaufman, 2020) understands the high stakes involved and feels the liberty to lead this thought-provoking process. The whole-person principles of the self-actualized individual provide the impetus and guardrails for extensive community involvement in a problem-solving exchange. Social interaction reigns and plays a pivotal role designing the activity at hand (Lave & Wenger, 1991).

Social investment in problem-solving enables us to observe active participants engaging with their community (Guerra, 2016). Lave (1993) makes a directed point with the following statement, "Theories of situated activity do not separate action, thought, feeling, and value and their collective cultural, historical forms of located, interested, conflictual, meaningful activity" (p. 7). These interactions describe situated practices in which people who acknowledge their differing thoughts and experiences continue to invest in collaborative problem-solving. Together, they synthesize the social-relational roles and shared a negotiated exchange (Linehan & McCarthy, 2000). While the "we" becomes the multiplied quality across the participants, the "whole person," functions as a self-actualized individual.

Contextualizing self-actualization as a key component within the whole-person principles, we pause to consider Kaufman's (2020) expanded research on Maslow's (1943) work. Kaufman sought to gain a deeper understanding of Maslow's concept of self-actualization. Upon Maslow's death, Kaufman contacted the Maslow family, knowing that Maslow was still developing his thoughts on his management theory. Working with Maslow's family, Kaufman researched Maslow's self-actualization work to discover that Maslow had a specific goal. Maslow explained his desire to prove that humans were capable of something greater than the negative manifestations of life (war, prejudice, and hatred) as he asserted that there is no intrinsic reason everyone should not be self-actualized. Kaufman expanded on this thought, clarifying self-actualization as an achievement and a base for further development.

RDM events can benefit from utilizing this self-actualized foundation. Self-actualized problem-solvers come together working as a community to share these personal assets (Maslow, 1943):

- Self-actualized problem-solvers process information with ease and tolerate the uncertainty of a complex challenge.
- They accept their own "self" and respect the "self" of others.
- They are spontaneous in abstract thought and objective.
- Self-actualized problem-solvers are problem-oriented, not person or self-focused.

REVISIT OF LIBRE MODEL ETHICAL PROBLEM-SOLVING

All problem-solving introduces vulnerability and risk to the problem-solver(s). Those involved in problem-solving will express their thoughts, feelings, and potential behaviors. Problem-solving in a group or community setting amplifies and heightens the stakes. Responsible Decision-Making is a component of The LIBRE Model (Listen, Identify, Brainstorm, Reality Test, Encourage), beginning with ground rules and check-ins on ethical and cultural competency. Reframed as a self-actualized whole person, working to offer their "Best" with others who are making that same commitment. The problem-solvers must adhere to the following principles:

- **Be Respectful:** Agree to encourage interpersonal care in problem-solving within a cultural framework judging people is unacceptable.
- **Values and beliefs:** Welcome and respect participants' views as they represent the problem-solver's cultural, cognitive, social, and emotional "self."
- **Safe:** Well-defined and specific boundaries established, ensuring everyone feels comfortable participating.
- **Confidentiality/Defined learning:** Confidentiality is respected care not to carry brainstormed thoughts outside the exchange to be humorous. The exchange parameters must be determined before any problem solvers (PS) exchange begins (Guerra, 2016, 2009; Guerra et al., 2024).

The RDM consultative and collaborative event involves decision-makers, planners, action-takers, evaluators, and those other persons directly or indirectly affected by the executed plans. Caring for oneself and caring for the community are essential factors. The LIBRE Model (2009a) reflects a collaborative need perspective.

IMPETUS TO THE LIBRE MODEL APPROACH

To better appreciate the value of a community-managed (RDM) problem-solving event, I outline the sequence of events that led to the development of the LIBRE Model. This context helps us understand the unique RDM contribution in addressing a challenge. One day, I received a call from a colleague who explained that, after considerable time and investment, a collaborative community materialized to assist public housing residents with the daily challenges. Unfortunately, shortly after beginning this noble initiative, the well-intended colleague experienced challenges among themselves as city-wide partners. He found himself spending more time in side-bar conversations rather than on the intended work. As he listened, he identified the challenges as coming from within and among the volunteer professionals. Each nurse, social worker, pastor, counselor, and community worker expressed a willingness to assist and share their knowledge, unique professional background, and training. As the collaboration became operational, each saw the problem and resolution differently. Their problem-oriented resolutions fit their unique professional skills and expertise. The diverse perspectives represented in the group tend to fracture the unified voice in selecting solutions and options to resolve the issues. The collaboration ceased to function smoothly, posing a threat to the viability of solutions. The lead author received a call for intervention to resolve the collaborative challenge. The result was the development of a decision-making model, the LIBRE approach, which focuses on collaborative and targeted resolutions. It is a community-friendly approach shared in a common problem-solving language allowing lay people to fully and equally participate.

Relational Problem-Solving Exchange

Over the last 23 years, young and old, in both English and Spanish used the LIBRE approach. One example was a public housing wife confronted with her husband's dual life and infidelity. The couple had been married for 28 years; he lived in Texas, and she was in Mexico. After all their children had married, she decided to move to Texas to live with her husband. What she found was that her husband had a parallel family in Texas. Although that relationship had ended, he had a 16-year-old daughter living with him from that parallel family (Guerra, 2009). The LIBRE Model was employed with prompts to structure the exchange and empower them to identify the problem. She relayed her story as she had experienced it. She walked away from the supportive listening exchange, but she had neither a solution nor anything else to offer. The counseling staff that had explained the LIBRE Model and problem-solving process thought they would never see her again. However, much to our surprise, she returned. She still had the provided LIBRE Model graphic and carefully pulled it out of her purse. Even as she cried, she urged the community of people that she had rallied to continue helping her address this complex challenge. She returned home to Mexico, consulted her married children, spoke to her husband, the young teen who called her husband, and her father. She had also taken the time to think about herself and her wants and desires. She explained how much she still loved her husband. This time, she walked through the door, ready to brainstorm and engage in a reality-testing process. She, now a problem-solver, took a deep breath as she completed the reality-testing step.

The LIBRE facilitator offered her the last step, Encourage, explaining that this was the time to develop her plan. She would stay in Texas with her husband and ask him to communicate with the young teen. She knew it would not be easy, so she decided to remain with her husband. She knew the interim decision was a short-term accommodation. Her mantra was, "I can do this."

In returning to our RDM event, use the same LIBRE Model steps, beginning with the "Listen and List" prompt. The difference lies in the increased complexity of communication involving others and the safeguarding of trust (Guerra, 2009). It is essential to reiterate that problematic discussions can introduce vulnerabilities associated with stages of development and life experiences. Take diligent care to listen before speaking and monitor all steps in the problem-solving process and honor the group's contributions.

OPEN TO COLLABORATIVE LISTENING

The RDM team opens communication, demonstrating a willingness to listen. Ways to demonstrate openness vary, from the way we sit to the uncrossed arms to facial expressions. Being open requires self-regulation, which, in turn, requires self-awareness. Attending to one's self-awareness entails paying attention to our thoughts, feelings, expressions, and words. By cultivating self-awareness, we can better regulate our listening, maintain self-confidence, and, as controversy arises, remain open to hearing, listening, and processing thoughts even if they are not in line with our own.

Willingness to Hear Different Perspectives

Without intending to become too involved, we often find ourselves drawn closer to those who share our views and, by extension, tend to shy away from those who hold different perspectives. Within the RDM exchange, all shared plausible ideas value opinions, thoughts, and expressions to be reality tested. Acceptance is a strong word; however, if the goal is to identify the best solution, then listen and consider all perspectives. At times, divergent thoughts prevail in identifying the best solution. A word of caution: pruning away thoughts too early in the process can derail valuable information, ideas, and creative thought. The Mexican wife not only needed to listen to herself, but she also needed to listen to her husband, her grown children, and her young teenager. It was then that she understood the value of different perspectives.

Listening to Those Who Are Different

A self-actualized person who is authentically present and actively participating, will listen to others, regardless of their opinions, to embrace potential learning, exploration, and discovery of innovative ideas. Everyone wins when listening is a shared value, and being self-aware maintains a sense of security. Let us imagine a fellow journeyman warning us that if we continue this same path, we will eventually see a large tree blocking access to the road. We have several options. We can ignore an untrustworthy person due to appearance and foreign accent. Prejudice and differences could easily disrupt the effectiveness of the problem-solving process. Or we can thank the person and consider the information offered. We can modify our path or ignore shared information. The quality of something unique and different is not always determined as good or bad. Staying receptive and open-minded, we increase the possibility of gaining valuable insights and understanding.

Respectful and Valued Exchange

According to Kaufman (2020) and Maslow (1943), self-actualization serves as a foundation for the greater good and the best that you can be. Sharing your "very best" with others invites the "very best" in what they will share, and collective achievement will be a greater good, better than what any of us could have achieved alone (Kaufman, 2020). A parallel thought applies to RDM. Listening to others who share a similar problem with different ideas can enhance our community's collective thinking and lead to greater benefits, even if we do not personally agree with the solution. One can get a greater gain when an exchange is based on respect and value.

MENDOZA FAMILY AS COMMUNITY EXAMPLE

The success in their family management and exchanges remained consistent with their values, traditions, and culture. The Castillos and Mendozas prospered in Mexico, and Teodosio extended their family business success. He established communication with other farming families. As Teodosio spoke with a neighbor about his 11 sons, 1 daughter, and his wife, he shared his thoughts and feelings about the importance of owning land in an unfamiliar environment. In discussions with Augustina, they decided to begin buying land, which now gave their family options outside Mexico.

Meanwhile, Augustina continued to work the family businesses in Mexico with her parents, sister, and children. The positive return of their son brought the family the recognition that the way they had conducted their business would have to change. Their listening and collected information signaled the difficulty they would face.

In Mexico, with the recent election, war, and rebellions, Pancho Villa was just one of the militant groups promising the people a new way of living and hope for the future. While the political climate was changing in Mexico, in Texas, the Texas Rangers were randomly killing Mexicans. This political climate meant that Texas would not offer the safe refuge they were seeking. The family was facing a challenge that would impact each one individually, as well as all of them collectively. Neither staying in Mexico nor moving to Texas provided the security and safety that they were seeking. An alternative option was a return to Spain; however, the elder Castillos were the only ones interested in this move, given its implications. The two Castillo daughters had been born in Mexico. The Mendoza mother and children were Mexican citizens by birth.

The first step in responsible decision-making problem-solving includes listening, and that is precisely where they invested their time and energy. The family continued to listen closely to the people they encountered. They listened to the merchants in the small towns, people who had now become their friends and allies. They listened to the priests and the church families. They asked questions and were attentive as they heard of experiences and ongoing actions. The more information gathered, the greater the clarity of the problem's naming.

STONES OF REMEMBRANCE

Listening is the first and most critical skill that is honed with attentiveness. Collaborative Listening involves many with guidelines to listen and boundaries not to interrupt, becoming more important as conflict arises within a community. Listening to the details of what was occurring helped the problem-solvers understand the context surrounding the problem. Learning took place in those quiet listening spaces as these self-actualized individuals came together to share the valuable information collected from across their communities.

CHAPTER 8

IDENTIFIED CONCERN

Envision the difficulty in naming a complex problem. The collective involvement of affected actors/people intensifies the struggle due to the diverse viewpoints and opinions shared by the group (Guerra, 2016). To set the stage for this chapter's discussion, we return to the Mendoza family story, as it celebrates the release of their grandson, son, and brother. The oldest brother questions, "What were you thinking? Do you know of the trouble you caused? Don't you care about anyone other than yourself? Now we are all at risk, and just because you wanted an adventure." A younger brother quickly remarks the obvious, "He is a kid, just like all of us; do not be so hard on him. He told you that he had wanted to go into the larger towns to see what was happening." While the teen's maternal grandmother cries softly in the background, Mama Tina (Augustina) speaks in an authoritarian voice, "That is enough. We are all here and safe. Let us give God thanks for what we have. We have each other, and yes, we have a problem." Coming right behind her is Papa Teo (Teodosio), who in his determined voice commented, "Yes, we have a problem, and thanks to God, we are all here safe. Let us remember who we are and bring our best thinking forward. We must decide on the problem we want to address. Each of you is free to speak, but you must also be willing to listen to one another. We will not criticize each other. Whatever we decide to do will impact each of us; we are a family, and we need to remember who we are and know that God is with us."

This complex event underscores the importance of responsible decision-making in achieving collaborative outcomes with broad implications (Guerra & Bollinger, 2011). Noteworthy was the immediate freedom the

From Problem-Solving to Responsible Decision-Making,
pp. 81–86
www.emeraldgrouppublishing.com

brothers expressed their differing opinions and perspectives. The adults listened. Once the young voices presented their views and perspectives, the parents spoke. In listening, we affirmed the shared values and their commitment to each other. The older brothers vented but never moved away from their family commitment to their younger Mendoza brother. Mama Tina spoke about the values that defined them as individuals and as a family and asked them to think about their primary concern. Mama Tina and Papa Teo held leadership roles in their family's lives, work, and in this problem-solving discussion. Their tone, manner, and the words they used were critical in managing the emotions and thoughts shared during their discussions. Their roles and positions in the family were critical to the values of their family. In this chapter, we will follow the transition involved in the problem-solving process. Practical communication skills, combined with high-level self-awareness and social awareness, help integrate the value of community into the problem-solving process. The group shared and exchanged nuanced information as it deliberated and thought-out plans for the problem-solving set of activities.

APPLIED SOCIAL AND EMOTIONAL SKILLS TO RESPONSIBLE DECISION MAKING (RDM)

Below is a list of five key life-impacting skills that are important to everyone investing in self-development. The list includes self-awareness, social awareness, relational skills, self-management, and responsible decision-making. We provide an example and invite you to participate in an activity to plan actions towards improved self-development. Start by stating your mantra and follow up with brainstorming and reality-testing activities that form the crux of your action plan. The Collaborative for Academic, Social, and Emotional Learning (CASEL, 2003) released research and resources for educators and interested people to use in working with children, youth, and adults. This CASEL group addresses the importance of self- and social skills, offering consumers examples, exercises, and activities to highlight the following skills learned:

Self-awareness involves recognizing and valuing one's uniqueness. Self-monitoring scrutinizes, safeguards, and ensures a flow of investment in self-awareness. For example, I feel uncomfortable as I enter a crowded room. My insight becomes my awareness. I can now manage myself effectively based on the information that I have acquired from this awareness. My mantra transforms my beliefs and becomes my goal and life compass: Toward a life in **Self-awareness:** *I am special and unique; I have the power to change; and I have the motivation and the power to influence other lives.* Use the LIBRE model to develop your action plan.

Social awareness involves the application of self-monitoring skills in group settings. Social awareness implies empathy and a connection with others' feelings, emotions, and perspectives. For example, I intentionally go into a social gathering with a problem-solving orientation. I automatically relate, understand, endure, and associate with their viewpoints, orientations, emotions, and roles in society. My mantra is my goal and my life compass: Toward a life in **social awareness:** My mantra is *Do unto others, what you want them to do unto you*. Use the LIBRE model to develop your action plan.

Relational skills involve communication skills in working with others. For example, I realize that I do not work well with large groups. Relational exchanges require me to acquire additional active listening skills to help me focus on what other people are saying. I watch other people feel more comfortable knowing they are heard. I, too, can relax now that I have increased skills that apply to other social exchanges. My mantra is my goal and my life compass: Toward a life with **Relational Skills:** My mantra is *Deep listening heals; do it with a receptive and open heart and mind*. Use the LIBRE model to develop your action plan.

Self-management involves skilled use of personal strategies to work alone or with others on tasks requiring an outcome. For example, I have a project that is due tomorrow. I take a deep breath, look around, and assess my commitments, the time needed, and what the project requires. Without losing sight of my needs, I develop a timeline and specific plan to complete it. Involves skilled use of personal strategies in working with others and/ or alone on tasks requiring an outcome. My mantra is my goal and my life compass: Toward a life with **Self-management and self-discipline:** My mantra is *Life is a path, and a journey, self-management and self-discipline are my linkages; resilience, persistence, perseverance, and goal setting are my drivers*. Use the LIBRE model to develop your action plan.

Responsible decision-making involves the management of complex problem-solving with multiple consequences to people. I am learning to work with others through observation and monitoring myself. A biblical story of the two prostitutes provides a graphic example. The complex problem is one baby and two mothers. The two women go to Solomon, demanding a resolution. While quite unorthodox, he listened and found the concern that involved one baby and two mothers. At once, he asked for his sword, realizing that the birth mother would rather have her child live with the other mother who had lost her child. Solomon meanwhile observed the other woman, who agreed "Yes, cut the living baby in half." She favored sharing the grief she was experiencing in having lost her baby (I Kings 3:16-18).

A problem-solver's level of social, emotional skills often attributed to self-actualization has an impact on quality and responsible decision-making

(Maslow, 1943) and on human agency (Bandera, 1986). The community, comprising of socially aware individuals, implemented relational skills to foster open communication, actively listen, and engage in complex problem-solving. Listening continues to be a primary and prerequisite skill by the community. For the Mendoza family, the questions were, "Should we go? Do we need to go? Should we stay? Do we need to stay?" My mantra is my goal and my life compass: Toward a life with **Responsible decision-making:** My mantra is *Responsibility means quality and carries consequences; No downsides, just benefits, it is a win-win situation in Life*. Use the LIBRE model to develop your action plan.

Identifying the Collaborative Primary Concern as a Question

Papa Teo and Mama Tina listened to their children, family, church and community friends, workers, and associates, and all offered information and/or opinions. The more they heard, the more they realized that moving from Mexico would be a more promising investment for their family. The primary question would take time to develop. Meanwhile, Mama Tina's parents and older sister listened and processed the same available information, which led them to a different decision. They still had one additional option: as they began their problem identification, they could return to their home of origin. For this text, the Castillo family used the LIBRE Model to process and identify the problem; however, it was not the same problem that the Mendoza family identified.

Identifying a problem and naming a goal involves several key factors: values and beliefs, consideration of the information collected, feasibility, and the potential benefit for all. The foundation and alignment of the identified focus on problem-solvers' values, beliefs, and standards, both as a family and among parents within the community, are crucial. All people involved in the problem identification shared freely diverse views, precepts, and beliefs that molded the context for interpreting the problem. For example, the Mendozas considered family as a fundamental and cherished value. While none of their 12 children were yet married, one of their sons had already proposed and was committed a young lady he loved. He had spoken to the widowed mother of the young lady about his intended commitment to her, which also included a commitment to care for the future mother-in-law.

Conversations and interactions with churchgoers, family members, business associates, workers, and patrons provided the contextual information required to identify the problem. All incoming news contributed to the family's dilemma as they pondered the feasibility and control of the identified problem. The Mendoza family worked with their identified constraints; their engaged son had already informed them of his intentions. All the Mendoza sons and daughters had been born in Mexico; Spain had no vested interest in them. Papa Teo had been traveling back and forth to Texas, had already purchased land, and had made acquaintances with people who could assist them. Texas was a more realistic consideration. The final factor in considering the move to Texas was the economic potential for each of them. Their contemplations examined their values and beliefs, as well as the information and feasibility. The identified problem-solving embodied their thoughtful consideration and merit to the two different proposed directions.

The problem/challenge identified for each of the two families leads them in different directions. While they shared the same information and values, two distinct problem directions emerged. Family roots, birthplace, childhood experiences, and self-awareness fueled a divergence in values and opinions which were couched into different realities experienced throughout their lives. Consequently, the focus on the shared information and values meant that the two families would face different challenges. For the Castillos, they addressed their return home to Spain. For the Mendozas, their identified concern was "How to plan their move to Texas."

SUMMARY

Collaborative Listening is the first step. Care to hear and allow all to speak is imperative. While identifying the problem appears to be an end in and of itself, it now leads to the next level of processing work involving brainstorming and the identification of realistic and non-realistic options. The problem-solving group had time to prioritize and eliminate options that were incompatible with the collaborative goal. For example, leaving the engaged son behind in Mexico was an inconsistent option with the goal of family unity. Critical decisions were made after problem-solvers submitted solution options for reality-testing. The values, respect, trust, and cultural tenets of the community continued to be the primary foundation and trust. The next chapter will examine the brain-storming and reality-testing steps of the LIBRE problem-solving exchange.

Identifying a collaborative concern is skillfully complex second step. While a goal-oriented concern urges immediate community action, each stage of the responsible decision-making LIBRE process affords time for reflection and thought. For instance, the two families needed time to think, pray, and discuss their distinct concerns and the implications. Value, beliefs, and communicated care guided both families and their extended communities, as they realized they could no longer live and work together.

STONES OF REMEMBRANCE

Open and safe communication is welcome and imperative for communications that hold weighted consequences. Each person within a family is socially and emotionally responsible for self. All should feel free and supported as they express their thoughts. Sharing values and thoughts respectfully in relationship one with the other is important. The community involved in their problems heard and valued what everyone had to say.

CHAPTER 9

PROCESSING RESPONSIBLE DECISION-MAKING

Brainstorming and Reality-Testing

The Mendoza and Castillo family problem-solving challenges provide the background for a discussion of brainstorming and reality-testing of solution options. The families shared the same situational context and environmental experiences in business and social settings; however, two distinct problems emerged when they came together to discuss their shared emerging challenges. Their family values and community input made the problem-solving an exceedingly challenging effort, as the Castillos saw the evolving process directing them to a return to their homeland, Spain. In contrast, the Mendozas focused on their move to Texas. The families faced two different challenges with brainstorming and reality-test options that would take each to distinct final directions.

According to historical records, the daunting premonition of the Pancho Villa event hastened all these moves which occurred with in a year. The families did not have time and moved quickly to remain safe. As they began brainstorming and reality-testing, a sense of urgency prevailed, and both families hastily moved through the problem-solving steps. Each family implemented a responsible decision-making process to address their distinct identified problem. As we continue to delve into the analysis of options, we will compare problem-solving individually as a single person versus as a group or community.

From Problem-Solving to Responsible Decision-Making,
pp. 87–91
www.emeraldgrouppublishing.com

INDIVIDUAL TO COLLABORATIVE PROCESS DISTINCTIONS

Differences exist between self-managed and collaborative tasks. Self-managed problem-solving and collaborative RDMs have distinct roles that contribute to the authenticity of the processes. We begin with a discussion of the differences between self-regulated and socially regulated learning (Hadwin et al., 2011) in the context of problem-solving tasks. An individual-managed problem is a one-person processed event solely owned. For example, once the Mendoza workers returned home to inform Augustina of the news that her young son had decided to join Pancho Villa. It was Mama Tina who initiated the problem-solving event. She immediately summoned her husband and, working with the cultural mores of the day, managed and executed the problem-solving plan. In an individual problem-solving event, it is the individual who monitors the process and strategically applies relevant data and information to develop an outcome that meets the defined goal.

In collaborative problem-solving, it is the group that regulates the application of the event and outcome. The identified problem goal is set and managed by the problem-solvers. Collaborative or shared learning allows for is interdependently regulated (Hadwin et al., 2011). This approach represents a collaborative and regulatory process whereby collaborators discuss and collectively participate in all decisions throughout the problem-solving process. Adaptations require unanimity; otherwise, the shared event ends. The Castillo and Mendoza families embody the concepts where the changing environmental risks and context strategically manage and regulate the incoming data and news to achieve different goals. The two families parted, with one group selecting to return to Spain and the other family focused on relocating to Texas.

The Mendoza family formed a new team to initiate the decision planning process. Hadwin et al. (2011) shared that regulated learning involves "collective adaptation and regulation of the collaborative processes; the team shares the monitoring, evaluation, and adaptive processes" (p. 67). Hadwin and colleagues suggest that there are "regulatory episodes" to move the group as a team to reinforce their collective interest and engagement. Returning to the story to illustrate this point, the Mendoza family, consisting of 11 sons and 1 daughter, and their parents reiterated the family needs and negotiated for a team reflecting different developmental ages, stages, and experiences. For example, one of the adult Mendoza men planned to get married and was prepared to stay behind. As the parents consulted with him in a sidebar discussion, they asked him to consider the dangers of his plan and committed to support him in returning to marry. Teodosio would return with his son to Mexico to marry and bring the young bride and her widowed mother to come to live with them in Texas.

The difference between individual and collaborative processing lies in the inherent complexity of involving and converging diverse points of view, as reflected in collaborative processing. With a shared experience approach, each problem-solving step requires teamwork when planning and processing actions. The demands and experiences of the problem-solving process apply to the collaborative brainstorming used to generate options and alternatives, and, with reality-testing, assist in sorting and prioritizing thoughts (Guerra et al., 2011). The LIBRE Model graphically organizes the discussion, which now shifts to focus on collaborative brainstorming (Guerra, 2009).

COLLABORATIVE BRAINSTORMING

Divergent thinking is at the core of group brainstorming. Through brainstorming, the problem-solvers hypothesize distinct options to address the identified problem. The goal is to be as creative as possible in designing diverse plausible and implausible solutions (Almutairi, 2015). A sense of improbability restrained the consideration of creative options. Reality testing will expand the thoughts that occur during brainstorming. While brainstorming acknowledges emotional expression, it is a time to encourage childlike thoughts, often lost as adults; it is an opportunity to make "wild-out there" solution options. Remembering the kindergartner who said, "I could get a monkey to bite the coach," he realizes from the brainstorming that he has gained a sense of self-control. In this case, the brainstormed options were in response to the identified problem, "how to plan their move to Texas." All fourteen voices representing their community expressed their creative solutions to the challenge and acknowledged and recorded their thoughts.

Brainstormed options that embraced family values and beliefs, providing a shared cultural foundation for this interactive communication. Brainstorming in the community is a safe time to explore diverse thoughts without judgment. For a community as diverse as the Mendozas, sustained attention in listening to each of the options was productive. Only after a period of family discussion were they ready to refine their expressed thoughts and ideas. This brainstorming activity allowed for divergent and creative thinking to spur other, more creative, realistic thoughts that led to innovative options.

The collaborative group now begins to prioritize developed options, allowing everyone to participate in a lively activity to refine their thoughts further. Eliminated option "too wild" to consider required placing an "x" or a line through the item, allowing a moment to pause, reflect, and revisit the emerging list of group-generated options. Once we completed and affirmed this brainstorming milestone, the group moved forward to reality-testing.

COLLABORATIVE REALITY-TESTING

When in the community, the act of reality testing may decelerate to accommodate the meticulous examination of all prioritized options. Maintaining an unspecified pace may be necessary as the group considers the sorted items and behavioral interactions that will be part of the prioritized item. Warren (2018) addresses this type of processing as reciprocal determinism, in which shaping the individual's behavior occurs by a bidirectional interaction between the three domains of cognition, behavior, and the environment. Individuals considered, adopted, and aspired to resolve the challenge with consideration of domain impact. For example, they examined how the option of leaving Mexico would affect the family, considering behavioral actions and interactions. Before developing the ultimate departure plan, problem-solvers allowed discussions about who would impact what and what would happen to whom. What would leaving as a group involve? How would the engaged son support himself once in Texas?

In Summary

Processing a problem can be laborious, requiring time and patience. When multiple people are involved, the problem-solving process slows down to include breaks and sidebar conversations. Brainstorming and reality testing involve major metacognitive skills that require mental, emotional, behavioral, and psychological investments. A sustained investment, however, comes with countless returns. Hearing and considering what each participant has to say contributes to ensuring successful returns. The prioritized options impact all parties involved in the associated action, help in reaching the goal, and facilitate the completion of final planning (Guerra, 2016, 2015).

STONES OF REMEMBRANCE

Sustained attention in processing complex challenges is analogous to the demands required for preparing to bake. Selecting the correct ingredients and following the recipe closely offers a sense of security. The details of preparation and the baker's expertise determine the success of the dish, while mistaken and critical ingredients compromise the quality of baked goods. Rushing to finish the task increases the chances of producing a mediocre outcome. As farmers, the Mendozas were most aware of the importance of considering each element in time, from planting to care, which contributed to the quality of the harvested outcome.

CHAPTER 10

RESPONSIBLE DECISION-MAKING

Encouraged to Plan

The collaborative brainstorming and reality-testing culminate in a journey that can be exhaustive and emotional yet refreshing. All have been involved. Each spoke, and they all heard and listened. The calmness that follows allows the team to take a breath of relief before moving to the final planning phase. The time has arrived for responsible decision-makers to gather and create an action plan. The final work encouraged the team to develop a path that delineates actions, necessary resources, and timelines, providing a structure to reach the shared goal. The overall collaborative process of responsible decision-making has led to this celebrated accomplishment, with the implementation of a well-defined plan of action. This step is the E-encourage step of the LIBRE Model.

Experiencing relief from engaging in a problem-solving activity that led to a responsible decision-making effort, the Mendoza and Castillo families felt more at ease with an optimism for a brighter future and its possibilities. They welcomed the pause for reflection on the methodical process that planned their near future. This closely knit family clan formed through marriage envisioned and pursued two distinct directions. Augustina's parents and sister would return to their homeland, and it was most unlikely they would ever see the Mendoza family again. The 12 young Mendoza siblings, in contrast, were ready for adventure. The lucrative investment in land catered to the adventurous fancy of the Mendoza family. By the time they finally finished their move, they already owned land in Texas.

From Problem-Solving to Responsible Decision-Making,
pp. 93–97
www.emeraldgrouppublishing.com
Copyright © 2025 by Emerald Publishing

Teodosio had started collegial friendships that enabled and hastened their decision to move to Texas.

ENCOURAGE

As noted earlier, the LIBRE Model (Listen—Identify a concern—Brainstorm—Reality-test—Encourage) graphic organizer helps problem-solving collaborators stay focused (Guerra, 2015). Note that two "limes/legs" of this final activity are in the LIBRE Model stick figure (Guerra, 2009). The left leg addresses the "Best steps to the plan." Beginning with this prompt, the problem-solving team will now focus on the identified challenge and goal. Additionally, the LIBRE Model action plan lists in chronological order the specific steps and allows for benchmark monitoring (Guerra, 2016). The detail involves identifying the responsible participants for each action step. In this way, problem-solvers develop various action steps, acknowledging the importance, value, and commitment to the plan. Each implementation step includes decision actions and identifies individuals who are responsible. The resultant strategic problem-solving pathway provides problem-solvers with incremental knowledge about each action, information about themselves as responsible individuals, and information about their community values as they assume responsibility for the decision-making that has occurred and will occur. All have spoken, listened, heard, and processed this final plan; the remaining task is to process the agreed-upon shared contract. To illustrate, we begin with the Encourage step. This problem-solving section offers an outlined goal, anticipation, a new beginning, and a shared commitment to each other. Each problem-solver (PS) has reached a place and a space that is best suited to their individual and collective talents and skills. There is a job in developing a collaborative solution.

The "Encourage" section presents accountability tools and benchmarks for the developed plan. The chronological listing of planned actions parallels the creation of a grocery list. Yes, please write a list of the items you need. What happens when one leaves behind the list? "Oh no, I am at the store, and my grocery list stayed on the counter." Similar accountability consequences occur when an action has no one ready to assume responsibility for that action. Benchmarking sets standards for actions to take place and is critical for the success of any planned activity. "Best Action Steps" yield greater results when implemented under a designated executor and with measurable standards that detail specific actions. Timelines foster efficiency in completing the action steps and in benchmarking the quality of work.

Back to the left-behind grocery list, to add value to a simple grocery list, adding details is important, such as quantity, can size, serving size, prices, and labels. The collaborative problem-solving Encourage steps prompt the PSs to provide timelines with the names of the responsible PSs for the implementation of each proposed action. The Mendoza and Castillo families understood that they were embarking on an intricate and complex process. Please consider the two problem-solving goals that these two families identified from the same social setting; each identified a distinct goal with both immediate and future consequences for their lives. Records indicate that Teodosio secured a green card and had already begun to buy land for their family. Now that they decided it was too dangerous to stay in Mexico, they moved more quickly to Texas, where they built homes for the families to join them.

The collaborative, responsible decision-making exchange closes with the development of a mantra or remembrance of their shared problem-solving exchange. Mantra functions as a rallying call or unifying impetus to go forward with the agreed upon "charge." For example, "With God, all things are possible." The plan is set. The mantra anchors the community's values and commitment to responsible decision-making with the active participation of all involved.

As we conclude this chapter, a question format is used to present takeaways that are essential tools for a collaborative, productive, and practical problem-solving process.

- What is responsible decision-making (RDM)?

RDM is a coordinated group-led collaborative problem-solving exchange. The distinction of the RDM approach is that all support a unifying direction amidst the complexity of working across multiple needs and individuals (see Figure 10.1).

- What is the difference between straightforward problem-solving and collaborative, responsible decision-making?

The difference between the two approaches is (1) the complexity of the problem-solving task and (2) the number of people involved in the processing of the challenge. For example, if my problem is whether to take a trip this weekend or stay home. This is a straightforward single concern that involves only me. Advice and consultation will not significantly affect the outcome, as I will be the only person traveling; others' options or thoughts are not necessary for my final decision. This is a simple problem-solving event.

Figure 10.1

A Blueprint for Using the LIBRE Model in a Collaborative Problem-Solving Exchange

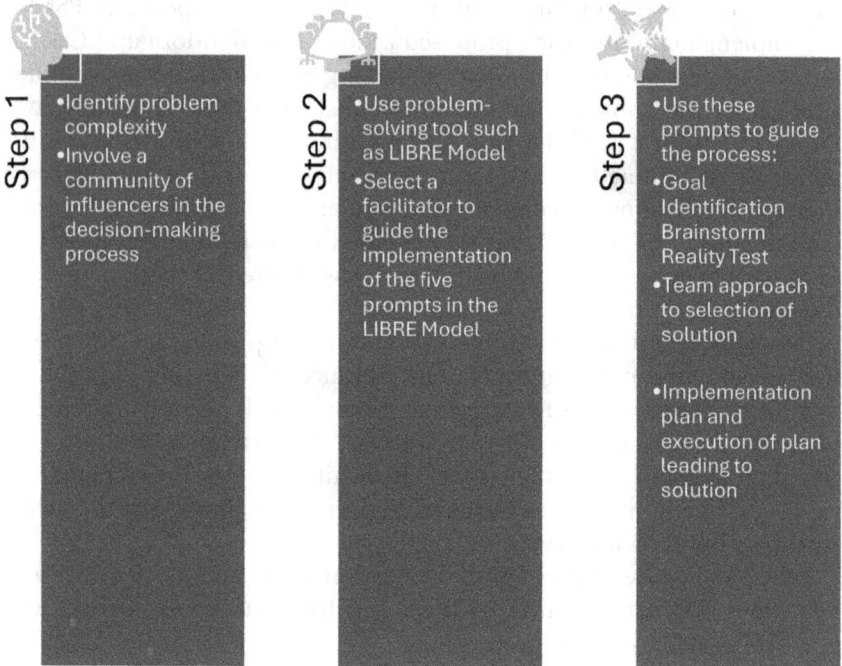

Step 1
- Identify problem complexity
- Involve a community of influencers in the decision-making process

Step 2
- Use problem-solving tool such as LIBRE Model
- Select a facilitator to guide the implementation of the five prompts in the LIBRE Model

Step 3
- Use these prompts to guide the process:
- Goal Identification Brainstorm Reality Test
- Team approach to selection of solution
- Implementation plan and execution of plan leading to solution

On the other hand, if the final decision involves my extended family and their availability to participate, their thoughts and options become important. A collaborative decision-making approach is imperative. The family's input, thoughts, and opinions become critical. Their participation ensures that more will benefit from the ultimate decision. The exchange becomes a shared communication, commitment, and ultimate plan (see Figure 10.2).

This chapter challenges us to consider the community and ask who contributes to the shared values within it. The focus is on the personal growth of the lead facilitator and the developmental growth experiences of all team members, as implied in this sample exchange involving the Mendozas. As you move into the space of responsible decision-making, the questions to consider are: Who will lead? Does the person leading the problem-solving exchange possess the necessary experience, skills, and reputation to keep the team together and ensure they follow? What are the shared values, and do they align with you and your team members?

Finally, self-in-identity is an important consideration that allows space for growth, change, and accommodation. "The best of me" and "the best

Figure 10.2

Differences Between Straightforward and Collaborative Decision Making

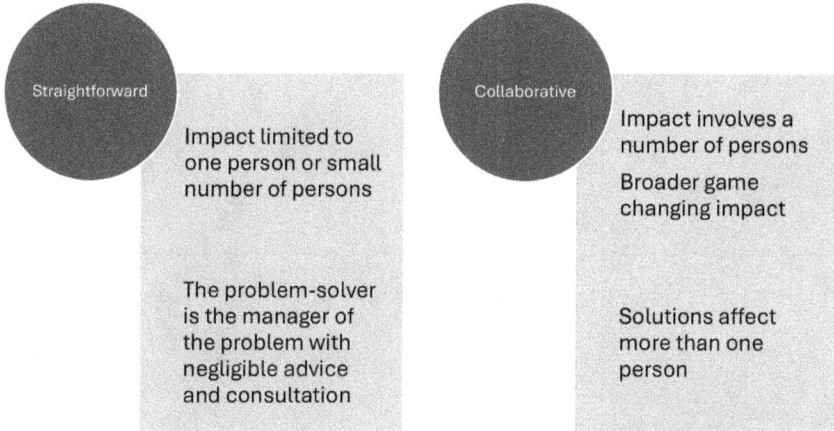

Straightforward

Impact limited to one person or small number of persons

The problem-solver is the manager of the problem with negligible advice and consultation

Collaborative

Impact involves a number of persons

Broader game changing impact

Solutions affect more than one person

of you" are maxims that reflect the integration of self in the community. Self-awareness and social awareness facilitate the addressing of complex challenges that encourage exploration, change, growth, and space, which are fundamental to effective problem-solving.

STONES OF REMEMBRANCE

Encouragement introduces closure to the problem-solving exchange. Time is allocated to all participants in the process to develop their shared solution plan. What is this task? The willingness to listen, hear, and value the other and manage the extent to which they share values. In collaborative, responsible decision-making, the stakes are higher, and so are the wins.

SECTION III

YOU IN YOUR JOURNEY

CHAPTER 11

PROBLEM-SOLVING TO RESPONSIBLE DECISION-MAKING STONES OF REMEMBRANCE

Since time immemorial, the widely researched subject is problem-solving. For instance, Aristotle paved his way to problem-solving through philosophical and pedagogical inquiry. The Gestalt theorists believed that the existence of a problem created a disequilibrium, an imbalance for the individual. Kurt Lewin, further to propose the importance of perceptions with "life space" to explain that persons need to create a cognitive balance, solution, to the presenting tension created from a problem or challenge. Others followed to ask basic questions that continue to guide problem-solving thinking, skill development, and efficiency. Questions explored include: (1) Who benefits from resolving a problem, and who should be involved in the resolution? (2) Why does it matter who resolves the problem? (3) How did the problem come about? And (4) What is the best way to resolve the problem? (Deckman, 2020).

Our actions, decisions, and behaviors determine who we become in this life. We are the agents of our lives, empowered and challenged to a self-awareness of freedom that will guide the decisions that facilitate who we will become. We will use this phrase as a reminder of "self " and as a backdrop to our discussion on problem-solving and responsible decision-making.

From Problem-Solving to Responsible Decision-Making,
pp. 101–111
www.emeraldgrouppublishing.com

This chapter provides a review of the problem-solving suggested approaches for addressing challenges of either straightforward or complex nature (see Table 11.1). Table 11.1 is an exercise for readers to apply problem-solving knowledge and skills in processing a personal complex problem requiring community input and participation. Complete this worksheet to demonstrate an understanding of the LIBRE Model. We are fortunate to have benefited from great problem-solvers, researchers, motivators, and individuals who shared their knowledge and experiences. We join these ranks as we invest in solving personal, societal, and professional (work-related) problems. Life is a journey filled with both simple and complex problems, and our competence in resolving these problems primarily defines our lives and impacts the lives of those around us. Problem-solving is an essential, life-changing process that varies from person to person. The ability to solve complex problems efficiently is one of the most sought-after skills in today's world. In this book, our journey provides a brief synopsis of key problem-solving concepts as presented in the LIBRE model, a widely used tool for solving both simple and complex problems. We offer this space for reflection and the expansion of innovative ideas. We provide a summary of the remembrances to summarize the basic steps in a systematic problem-solving approach. Furthermore, the "Stones of Remembrance" provides a summary of how we empower and invest in you as a self-actualized agent responsible for ongoing personal growth and self-development.

STONES OF REMEMBRANCE 1

In Chapter 1, we introduced two families, their core values and beliefs, and their lifelong experience with problem-solving. We provided examples of how their core values of church/ faith, culture, community, and trusting relationships shaped their problem-solving approaches. Self-awareness and their sense of responsibility to protect the welfare of communities are at the crux of this question: "What are the core and unifying tenets that define you, your walk, and life actions?" The invitation is to reflect on what defines and provides boundaries for actions.

STONE OF REMEMBRANCE 2

The focus is on self-development and managing substantial amounts of information. A core element in the rarely considered daily decision-making process is the shared phenomenon of Self. Considering the concept of self means empowering oneself to seek people and environments to help with

Table 11.1

A Worksheet to Plan the Identification of Plausible Solutions to a Problem-Solving Exchange Using the LIBRE Model

Suggested Guiding Questions Address Each LIBRE Model Prompts	Your Implementation Plan to Address Each Prompt (List activities/tasks to define how you will gather information.)	Timeline
Prompt 1: Listen and List: Identify discomfort cues (challenges you are experiencing) that define the problem to be addressed. Select one: ☐ Straightforward ☐ Complex		
Discomfort Cues Leading to a Problem – what is the context to the challenge? 1. What is not working for you? 2. Identify events, conversations, behaviors, and other cues that define the feeling of discomfort. 3. What is occurring within the environment that is creating a challenge 4. List these items.		
Discomfort Cues Leading to a Problem – what is the context to the challenge? 1. Identified with persons who are in your community, what is contributing to the feeling of discomfort. 2. As collaborative, list with those persons what the discomfort settings and/or events are. 3. With those same identified trusted persons include experienced challenges and ask willingness to participate in the PS process.		

(Table continued on next page)

103

Table 11.1 Continued

Prompt 2: Identify the problem (concern, goal, question) and determine whether to use a straightforward or a collaborative approach.	
Identify the Problem _____ 1. With a Collaborative Responsible Decision-making event - review the information gathered in the LISTEN stage. 2. Make sure you as a group agree with the problem stated. 3. The problem must be a single problem within the control of the group to manage and to solve.	
Prompt 3: Brainstorm (Define, describe, and list possible and impossible solutions to the problem.)	
1. This step encourages divergent and convergent thinking. 2. List all possible and improbable solutions to the identified problem. 3. Prioritize the most possible and probable solutions to the problem. 4. Now place an "X" by the impossible solutions to the problem. 5. Prepare those prioritized solutions for reality testing.	

(Table continued on next page)

Table 11.1 Continued

Prompt 4: Reality Test (Discuss and gauge the plausibility of solutions/behaviors that could solve the problem and select the preferred and most appropriate solution(s) to the identified problem/challenge.)

1. Begin with the number one prioritized solution and you will follow this same analysis with each of the prioritized options.
2. What would occur if I selected this option? Who besides me will be impacted? Will this solution create "healing or harm" in solving the problem with this option?
3. This review of prioritized solutions is evaluated on flexibility, replicability, attractiveness, affordability, convenience, and most of all, alignment with your personal and professional values, beliefs, culture.
4. Select the best option or combined options to then move forward to develop the action plan.

Prompt 5: Encourage (Select a solution and plan for success; the level of involvement in the planning and implementation will vary depending on the complexity of the problem and solution.)

1. Identify and celebrate the solution option(s) you have selected from the reality-testing step.
2. Revisit your identified problem and consider the problem as your goal endpoint.
3. List your action steps as they will need to occur.
4. Opposite each step, identify standards for the various implementation phases, including key milestones, needed resources, timelines, and key persons who can facilitate and assist the problem solver in success. Hence, you are formalizing your journey to success.
5. Review the action steps and identified timelines to accomplish major milestones.
6. As the last action to this exercise, create a Mantra to bring a remembrance to this commitment to create change.

Si se puede (I can do it) or as a Responsible Decision-Making collaborative

Mantra: _____ *En la unidad esta la fuerza* (Our strength is in our collaboration with others.)

105

that development. This practice includes setting aside time and space for personal notes, daily experiences, and self-reflection. Be ready and willing to pose questions about these experiences and be prepared to revisit or discuss those questions with trusted others later. Listen, notice individuals, and identify good listeners in your community. We are more likely to learn more and with greater depth when we learn in community with others through a team effort. To offer a perspective on the exploration of self, a friend decided he wanted to learn how to knit, so he went to YouTube, found a site, and carefully followed the instructions but I never considered the larger implications (context).

Proud of his newly acquired skill and needing practice, the hiker planned a trip. He would take a 4-hour flight, imagining that it would be an excellent time to practice. As he waited to board, an older lady approached him and asked if she could watch him knit. He responded, "Of course," she began to comment, "That is an unusual stitch, I have read about it but have never actually seen it before." He smiled, feeling quite proud of himself. She continued, "Honey, you are going so slowly with each stitch that you will not be able to finish at that rate." She then walked away. He was stunned. Is speed a contextual factor to consider?

He became concerned and realized he had missed a critical goal. The invitation is to find someone close to you who is a good listener and would be willing to safely walk and talk with you about exploring self-development. "Am I missing a skill that someone (outside myself) may see and help me person?"

STONE OF REMEMBRANCE 3

Chapter 3 describes the role of self in social settings to manage conflict and reflect on implications of problem-solving approaches. Similarly, development, drive, and resolution influence a problem-solver's self-awareness, a key factor in efficient decision-making processes. First, reflect on the question, how do we approach a conflict or challenge? Second, do we go out of our way to avoid a confrontation? When confronted with a need that must be met and managed, do we do our best to avoid it? For instance, someone decides to take a 15-mile pilgrimage, a daunting challenge for us. How would this hiker approach the challenge and prepare for the event? He felt that he would need a walking schedule. Without any more planning, he felt that by practicing daily for a month or so, he would prepare to walk the 15 miles successfully. The day came, and he started his journey. Did he effectively address the problems or issues associated with this daunting challenge? What problems or issues should he consider for a successful trip? As the walk continued, he gained a deeper understanding of himself.

Rather than stopping for water, he pressed forward. He did not want to be the one individual that had to stop. He wanted to keep up with the others. His drive to keep up with the rest of the hikers overrode his need to prioritize self-care and remain hydrated. Erikson saw individuals as having free will in all development, and it is critical to remember that in resolving each life-development crisis, we have access to self-developed informed possibilities. Bandura (1989) viewed individuals as agents of their actions and destinies, likewise, Erikson (1963) embraced the concept of free will in individual development. Life is changing, and so is the development of the hiker to become an efficient problem-solver. He needs to be open and consider these life lessons learned so he may use them in meeting and managing future challenges. What I learned was that I must pay attention to myself. If not me, then who? What is the challenge that you identify? Where are you in that challenge?

STONE OF REMEMBRANCE 4

Opportunities for developing relational skills while responding to the complexities of the human experience exist within the problem-solving community. While we share common events in the community, each person is a separate agent with distinct thoughts, self-identity, and experiences. To highlight these distinctions, we presented four engagement styles that are evident in our problem-solving approach. Each engagement style describes learned behaviors observed in problem-solving approaches. Human responses vary under unusual situations. A calm person, when faced with a crisis, will react and behave differently than an impulsive person. The Mendoza family, for example, once they realized that their son was potentially in great danger, immediately assumed a problem-solving, goal-focused style. However, family members will not always approach challenges using the same engagement style.

Engagement styles are consistent with the family traditions, values, and beliefs of a problem-solver. This presentation provides an increased appreciation for who we each are, our self-awareness, and what we offer others. We propose four engagement styles—potential, venting, goal-focused, or actual engagement to guide this discussion on interaction styles and their impact on the decision-making approach. Where do you see yourself? Where would you place yourself in the engagement styles framework? In what situations will you play different engagement roles? Would you prefer to engage differently? If so, what is the challenge in moving to a different engagement style? Would you have reacted differently if he had been your son?

STONE OF REMEMBRANCE 5

Personal investment is fundamental for achieving self-actualization. One must be prepared to remain at ease, nurture oneself, act, and engage in self-reflection. Self-awareness enhances developmental timelines and social interactions. Our investment and self-management decisions are personal and at our discretion. This is a moment to appreciate our identities, both as individuals and as constituents of our community. We are social beings, unique in potential, purposeful, and intentional. Understanding our "self," emotions, thoughts, and existence drives us toward a continuous state of reflection. We encourage you to reflect on the engagement styles and their role in routine and work-related issues. Which engagement style is most compatible with your preferred interaction style? Would you address the same situation in the same manner a second time?

STONE OF REMEMBRANCE 6

Life is not without challenges. A whole person (mind-body-spirit) with a problem-solving life-orientation is proficient in critical thinking skills. From one day to another, things and people change. Efficient problem-solving activities require a symbiotic relationship between a sense of self-awareness and proficiency in self-management. If we remain open to learning, we can become more discerning and skilled in interactions with others. How would you address an unwanted challenge? Describe how you see yourself in a troubling context, examine what is within your self-awareness, and control to manage.

STONE OF REMEMBRANCE 7

Listening is a critical and seldom-attended-to skill that is indispensable for the efficient problem-solver. As conflict's seriousness or problem increases, so does the importance of listening. Listening to the details of what is occurring helps to understand the conflict's context, its rapid development, and its interpretation by the affected person. The context is rich with information that can help pinpoint the contributing factors of the issue at hand. Still, quiet listening spaces help the self-actualized individual to be more efficient in reflective learning. Learning in community can be valuable when self-actualized persons feel comfortable sharing their reflective learned experiences. The best in a person, when shared with the best of others, produces a burst of creative and innovative ideas to address prominent issues. Do you consider yourself a self-actualized individual? What could you do to increase your sense of self-actualization?

STONE OF REMEMBRANCE 8

Open and safe communication is essential in naming and describing a challenge. It is important to identify and focus on conflict as a target, making clear communication a major and critical investment in the problem-solving process. Each person within each family is socially and emotionally responsible for themselves and accountable to the family and the community. The inclusion of other voices and viewpoints enriches and strengthens the brainstorming, reality-testing, and selection of the most functional and impactful options. Open and safe communication and active listening create a respectful and honoring environment that fosters collaborative decision-making. Naming the factors, including values, traditions, and beliefs, contributes to your self-identity. How have these values affected your problem-solving and making responsible decisions?

STONE OF REMEMBRANCE 9

Brainstorming and reality-testing of complex challenges are analogous to adding the main and correct amount of ingredients necessary to bake a successful treat. Selecting the proper ingredients and following the recipe closely offers a sense of security. The success of the dish is in the details of preparation and the baker's skill. The wrong ingredients compromise the quality of the baked goods. Rushing to finish the task increases the chances of ending up with a failed outcome. For the Mendozas as bakers, they were most aware of the importance of considering each ingredient; each element had the potential to affect the quality of the outcome. Within the collaborative responsible decision-making process, problem-solvers had time to listen, discuss, brainstorm, and reality-test (Guerra, 2015, 2016). How would you describe the steps you use to brainstorm and reality-test options? As a problem-solver, how do you assist and evaluate potential outcomes? Reflecting on a recent problem, how would you describe your brainstorming and reality-testing?

STONE OF REMEMBRANCE 10

Carrying the analogy forward, the bread is ready once cooked. Courage to act, to do, and to create positive changes toward new growth is not an easy task; a supportive group can help. The collaborative group offers their skill and willingness to listen, hear, and value the other people that they work with. In collaborative responsible decision-making, the stakes are higher, as are the wins. Even if the entire exchange is unsuccessful, there is always space to encourage those involved in communication. They may have had to compromise along the way, but the people involved within the community have a lasting commitment to how they treat each other and invest in problem-solving exchanges. How would you rate your communication skills in the community or with collaborators? What areas in communication would you like to invest in to be more effective as a problem-solver? Encouragement begins with yourself and then extends out to be a part in grooming a community that encourages others amid the complexities found there.

STONE OF REMEMBRANCE 11

Lessons well-learned and remembered nurture one's wisdom. Such was the case with the wealth of wisdom found in the Mendoza family, and they worked with their children to plan their move to Texas. Wisdom represents not only knowledge, but is the product of insights, reflections, critical thinking, openness to adaptability, and perceptions gathered to embellish the knowledge available for problem-solving. Wisdom blooms in the present, in the past, and is evident in decisions that have a positive and lasting outcome. Wisdom also flourishes when learning from our mistakes. The ability to juxtapose wisdom and knowledge emerges from lessons learned from every problem-solving event. This summary of reflection records the search for meaningful growth and development to ensure a far-reaching impact. How would you acquire the wisdom to use knowledge more efficiently in a problem-solving event? What examples of wisdom have you seen applied to problem-solving?

STONE OF REMEMBRANCE 12

This space allows you to share yourself and your story. Your story and the stories of others you have encountered provide context for impressions, engagement styles, and conflict resolution. Twelve "Stones of Remembrance" represent each of the 12 Mendoza siblings from the Castillo-Mendoza family legacies. Unfortunately, one of the 11 sons died of tuberculosis as a young man as he traveled back and forth coordinating business between Texas and Mexico. The remaining 11 siblings lived long lives.

As for me, I draft my story as one of Mendoza's great-grandchildren. My story, lessons learned, Stone of Remembrance, as a Mendoza family descendant, continue to reflect my values, faith, community, and the trust I learned in community. Remembrances I will always cherish.

CHAPTER 12

MY FAMILY RESPONSIBLE DECISION-MAKING EXPERIENCE

This chapter provides you space to reflect and record your introspective thoughts of your family's genealogy, values and beliefs, accomplishments, and attributes associated with their wisdom, experience, and developmental problem-solving. To accomplish this task, the following structure is offered: (1) begin by summarizing core experience(s) that have influenced you; for instance, significant values and traditions, (2) review key decisions made that contributed to your self-development, for example, takeaway lessons learned, and (3) outline your life Experience(s) that have contributed to your development, (4) chronicle your journey of living, growing, and continual transformation and (5) capture significant developmental problem-solving changes that have influenced you. Of significance is the role of agentic engagement, a willingness to show up and be present; reflections of your self-actualized best (Maslow, 1943) and your best for your family, friends, and community (Kaufman, 2020).

WHERE WE HAVE BEEN

Life is a constant path, shaping us in unique ways that define who we are over time. We all have our assets, values, and perspectives that influence where we have been. Our journey has "ups and downs," challenges, and

From Problem-Solving to Responsible Decision-Making,
pp. 113–121
www.emeraldgrouppublishing.com

opportunities. We can gain perspective and, at times, an advantage learning from others.

Throughout the book, we have explored problem-solving as an individual response to personal challenge(s) managed with personal problem-solving engagement styles and to address complex community challenges have explored collaborative responsible decision-making exchanges. The journey of self-discovery and growth is not just about understanding our past, but also about empowering ourselves to shape our future. Your vision and agency direct your future.

Looking to those who came before us for examples of values, experiences, challenges, and behaviors is a reflective exercise. We all experienced a less-than-perfect life; no family has ever been completely successful in its community affairs. Our family story provides us with the opportunity to learn from our predecessors. Once you identify values and define family assets, you can orient the awareness to evaluate and manage them. You can now understand and make an informed decision to agree or disagree with those values. Most importantly, you can now assess self-identity with a better understanding of our connected past. An ideal starting point to systematically and analytically study the challenge and make the best decision is now. Reviewing the context allows us the opportunity to compare the values and defined assets of our ancestors and explore their alignment with our values. Values inform the approaches to address conflict. Are there patterns of avoiding, ignoring, venting, or approaching challenge with intentionality? Yes, our ancestors' values and experiences influenced, to some degree, how we approach decision-making.

The LIBRE Model is a prompt-based conduit for approaching, processing, and developing resolution plans (Guerra, 2009a, 2009b, 2015, 2016). Two examples, (1) a straightforward exchange with the retrieval of young Mendoza and (2) a collaborative decision-making process with the Mendoza clan's move to Texas, show how each problem differs from the other. Similar prompts manage each time a new challenge appears. The number of collaborative actors and the complexity of the decision influence the pace and quality of the decisions. The outcomes yield insights that can inform our self-development, as well as that of our family and communities. The "Stones of Remembrance" detail learned lessons. Who we are and what we aspire to become begins as we observe others and interact with the community. These lessons learned are here for future reference as we walk our journey and invest in self-development. I humbly offer one more story, mine, as an example of a moment in time when I became engaged in a goal to study my ancestors' ways of approaching and solving problems. Their knowledge and success in solving problems became our model to use and improve.

MY STORY

I am authoring my story to you, my grandchildren, to honor my parents, grandparents, great-grandparents (Teo and Tina Mendoza), and all those in my life who tirelessly worked to provide me with the tools and the will to become a contributing, self-actualized professional. This context gave life to my learned life values. My personal and problem-solving development have successfully carried me forward.

Context

I begin with my mother, a second-generation Mendoza, raised in a wealthy family with loving parents and strong Christian values; their financial prosperity continued as descendants of landowner who grew and sold vegetables meanwhile renting large tracks of land to the local county for mineral rights. My parents and their families were part of the Depression, a time of ravaging impact on this country's economy to the point of destruction. The scarcity and shortages of life necessities had a deep impact on my dad's Guerra family, while the Mendoza descendants had food and continued their business endeavors. While the bakery did not continue, my mom and sisters fondly remember going to the ranch where they found an abundance of corn, okra, and other vegetables. They recall bringing home large quantities not only for themselves but also for neighbors and church families.

My parents met in high school and married during World War II. I am a Mendoza great-grandchild and Guerra descendent. As a young child, I met Mama Tina, but Papa Teo had passed by the time I was born. I have no memory of him; however, Mama Tina has a different recollection. She was a small, strong lady; small, thin, and sunbaked. It was clear that she was someone who spent a great deal of time outdoors. My grandfather was one of the 11 Mendoza men. Situated in the middle, he was not the oldest or youngest. Cruz married a young miss, Donicia Cortez, the only daughter of a family composed of a mom, dad, and two brothers.

My Contextual Values and Assets

My story begins with who I am, a proud Mexican American (two generations as U.S citizens). I, Dr. Norma Susan Guerra, am a golden strand of that embraced lineage and as a goal-focused person, my desire is to share learned wisdoms with you (my grandchildren). I begin with your great-grandmother Rosie Mendoza, Nanie-G, who was one of Cruz and Donicia's seven children. She, your great-grandma, had two brothers and five sisters. In terms of birth-order, she also fell in the middle just like her dad, two older sisters and a brother, and two younger sisters and a brother. The Mendoza values of family and church continue. As a young child, your Nanie-G spoke of how they would walk as a family to church. She said they would follow the train tracks as their path. Your great-great grandmother was active in church, taught Sunday school, sang in the choir, and was active in the women's sewing circle. Education was important to their community, and it was a value your great-grandmother embraced. My grandmother was one of my Sunday School teachers; I could hardly wait until I was in the third grade so I could move and be in her class. Education was and continues to be an important value and her lessons extended outsider the class as she taught me how to sew by hand, we made cross stitch aprons. Your great-grandmother wanted to go to college since she was a teenager. She had dreams of becoming a nurse, while her sisters left high school to marry and start their families, and her brothers joined the military and worked. She remained faithful to her education and was the only one in her family to graduate with a high school diploma, a major accomplishment she always cherished.

Your great-grandfather, too, was ambitious. He wanted to be the best printer and map maker in San Antonio. His family included his mother, father, and three brothers. Life was extremely difficult with your great-grandfather. Seasonally, he would leave school with his family to become migrant workers who picked cotton and other crops. In the middle of their family struggles, your great-grandfather's mother died. He met your great-grandmother in high school, and they enjoyed each other's company walking her home from school before he went to work. With the loss of his mother, his life changed. High school was difficult. His mother's passing disrupted all his plans, forcing him to take on his family's welfare after school. He was now responsible for his little brother and himself, as he continued to work after school. Everything within him called him to quit, but your great-grandmother insisted he continue going to school. She became his angel of encouragement, and she helped him through his terrible loss. Your great grandfather graduated from high school. He too was the first in his family to achieve this accomplishment.

Problem-Solving With the LIBRE Model

Your great-grandfather had a best friend in middle school and high school with whom he shared experiences working as a printer apprentice, playing, as well as going to school. They were remarkably close friends, but before I talk and share this friendship, I must tell you that one day your great-grandfather learned that his friend had a pretty cousin. Wow, seeing your great-grandmother, a distinguished young lady different from the other girls enthralled him, and immediately he fell in love. Once in high school, he became active in ROTC, and he dreamed of taking your great grandmother to the military ball, but how could he? Indeed, he had a real problem.

Your great-grandfather was a problem-solver. He listened closely to his head and heart and decided he would go to talk with his best friend's mother. Along with his best friend, they identified the problem as "getting Rosie's mom's permission to go to the ball." They brainstormed how best to ask your great-great-grandmother's permission to take her daughter, your great-grandmother, to the military ball. They had a large and animated discussion. Once his best friend and his best friend's mother had prioritized options, they reality-tested those options to further consider their plausibility. While they were ready to develop a plan, what they realized was this was no longer a one-person challenge, rather it would take a community to resolve this challenge.

Responsible Decision-Making With the LIBRE Model

A collaborative of community members used a responsible decision-making approach which was influenced contextually by a great-great-grandmother's mother who was extremely strict; a domineering person (she would be the person that he would need to talk with), and a pressing need for help from a friend and his mother. How did he resolve it? Do you have any ideas on how best to approach the problem? He decided to be direct, and with the help of his best friend and his mother, they developed a plan. His friend's mother, Mrs. Mendoza's sister-in-law, volunteered to first speak with your great-great-grandmother's mother and then he would introduce him. Your great-grandfather would then visit her and introduce himself. The plan worked; her parents agreed to let your great-grandmother attend the military ball. Their love grew. Your great-grandmother and great-grandfather graduated from high school. He then joined the Air Force with dreams and a plan for their future together.

One year later, they married and relocated to California, his station of duty. Your great-grandmother says that they were extremely poor. She had to live with little, despite her previous prosperity. She grew up in a household with enough food available. For the first time, she had to live with a scarcity of bread and other basic items. The difficulty she faced made the decision clear for them as a couple once she learned that she was pregnant—she would return home to San Antonio to give birth to me (your grandmother). I was born in July at Fort Sam Hospital. Her older sister, Tina (named after Mama Tina), drove the Mendoza women and your great-grandmother to the hospital, only to return with a new Mendoza-Guerra baby, me (your grandma, Nanie-G). Later in the day, your Great-Grandfather called and spoke with his brother-in-law Sam (one of your great-grandmother's brothers), who congratulated him, and informed him that he was now the father of a little girl.

Context to My Story

Soon after, your great-grandfather came back to San Antonio to pick up his wife and daughter. They all returned to the air force base in Riverside, California. Eleven months later, your great-grandmother gave birth to your esteemed granduncle. Years passed. Once my father, your great grand-father, served his country and completed his military time of duty, they returned home to San Antonio. While in the military, your great-grand-father continued to work within the printing business. When he returned to San Antonio, his brother-in-law, who worked at Ft. Sam Houston in the drafting section, and found a job announcement for a printer. He received an offer which he approved and was hired. Now, with a job, they bought their first house. Your great-grandmother explains that she wanted to move to the Southside of San Antonio, where the house prices were more reason-able. So off we went.

Self-Identity

I now share my interesting, rollercoaster adventurous life. Those were the days when we had our most trusted allies and greatest adversaries. Our neighborhood had vestiges of racial segregation. Children suffered the humiliation of name-calling coupled with insults denigrating where they lived or ate. Our best attempt at negotiation resulted in our parents ensuring we maintained close ties with our cousins and church for com-raderies. Friends, family, and church community affirmed our immediate family values, which helped us overcome the humiliation suffered because of my background, color of skin, and languages we spoke. Your great-grandfather and great-grandmother worked several jobs. To give you a glimpse of my early life, I would like to share one story about myself. I was insecure growing up when I was outside the home by myself. Throughout first grade and well into second grade, I cried every day after school. I would wait by the steps of the school crying while parents or relatives picked up the other children. In the second grade, your granduncle joined me on the school steps. I tried to explain, "You don't understand; she is going to leave us here—she is not going to come back for us."

Monday through Friday, these daily events unfolded in the same way—I cried, and each day, my brother and the school janitor would come to console me. The school janitor lady would come, console me, and eventually our mother would arrive. However, a fortunate event was about to occur; right across the street from our house, school officials were building a new elementary school. Wow! Freedom and independence occurred. We would walk to school and home—the problem solved. I began the third grade with renewed excitement, and after completing elementary school, moved on to middle school. Completing elementary school was a highlight event in my life because I had graduated and would be going to middle school. That was my first graduation. It was the janitor lady from my first elementary school. She came up to me, we greeted and hugged. Then she said, "You are the little girl who cried every day because your mother came late." "That is me," I responded. Now a mature pre-teen, I held tight to my new independence, identity, and security. I learned I could cry, do nothing, or I could problem-solve options. Problem-solving offered more promising results.

Responsible Decision-Making With the LIBRE Model

I will take you back to finish relating your great-grandfather's success story. Remember, he was the best mapmaker in San Antonio. He was proud of this accomplishment, which received special recognition. His efforts to be the best were paying off. As a civilian worker, he had been creating maps for the military until, one day, a military officer paid him a visit. Together, his boss and the military officer asked him if he would consider moving to Panama and making this his home base, so that he could consult with other countries. His expertise in topographic map-making became nationally known. They alerted us that he would travel to several South and Central American countries to teach and assist with map-making. Meanwhile, we (his family) would live in the Panama Canal Zone. They came to him with the invitation to travel, consult, teach, and help with map making at a much larger level than he had ever imagined.

He came home and spoke with your great-grandmother. Behind closed doors, there were many conversations; the challenge question involved whether to go. They brainstormed and reality-tested their proposed solutions to the issues at hand, inviting his brother, her sisters, and parents to weigh in. After fully exploring options, we moved to Panama; a new country, a new place to live, new schools. New experiences at church, community, education, and work were on the horizon. As a family, we experienced a global view of life and other cultures during our stay in Panama. When my dad's potential employer invited us to stay after completing the initial tour, and after much discussion, we returned to our roots in San Antonio. Through this new adventure, we learned to embrace new cultures, gained insights into diverse ways of life, and had unforgettable experiences along the way.

The family story places us with your beloved grandparents; these memories will continue forever as you and your families develop your self-identities. This is only a small sliver of your grandparents' and great-grandparents' lives in encountering challenges and change. This is an ideal segue for you to begin your narrative. As you use the LIBRE Model you will find that problem-solving is an investment and a tool designed to address personal and professional challenges.

Your story, with the help of family members, could bring you closer to searching for your ancestors' treasures of knowledge that could be lost forever. I hope my story provides the impetus to start your journey and adventure of a lifetime. Select a question you have and use the LIBRE prompts to assist your search for answers to your question. Start by completing Table 12.1 with the help of your friends or family. Consider an issue that has been troubling you or someone in your family. Identify it as a problem that needs a solution.

Remember that before working on a problem, ensure the problem is within your control and your power to solve it. Once you have outlined your problem-solving approach, share with your close friend or close family member so that they can be your partners in this journey. Bonne chance!

STONES OF REMEMBRANCE

Your story, your family, and your life experiences have made you the person you are, and as a result your shared wisdom and learnings are takeaways which your children will treasure and influence their lives as the next generation. Meaningful investment leads to the most powerful learning. Embrace and talk about the best in you; forgive the less-than-ideal to be a more self-actualized problem-solver.

Table 12.1

LIBRE Model Problem-Solving Plan

LIBRE Model Prompt	LIBRE Model Response
Listen and List Challenges you are experiencing.	Ex. Who or what family started the tradition of attending college? What prompted them to the need for a college degree? (This sample problem is provided to assist you in identifying your problem or issue that needs resolution.)
Identify A concern and record as a question.	
Brainstorm Unrealistic and realistic options, then prioritize and place an "X" by non-workable options.	
Reality-test Carrying over prioritized options, write-out, *"What would it look like if you (behaviorally) implemented that option?"* Then repeat the same question response to each prioritized option.	
Encourage (1) Record Best Steps.	
(2) Identify a Timeline for completing each step.	

Mantra:_____(Write a phrase that will remind you of the challenge you are about to begin.)

GLOSSARY OF TERMS

Actual engagement style refers to highly invested problem solver who actively listens, seeks input, and values collaboration. S/He/they consistently looks for and take(s) into account advice from collaborators and display(s) empathy toward those engaged in problem-solving discussions.

Cultural values are beliefs grounded in culture, inherited within families, and acquired individually. Common values often discussed to include religion-inspired faith, loyalty, gender-related practices, honesty, friendship, and ambition.

Encouraging problem-solving refers to investing time and effort in self-reflection while crafting a well-informed plan to overcome both simple and complex obstacles.

Goal-focused engagement style is characterized by being a decisive problem solver, taking prompt action, making informed decisions, and taking responsibility for one's actions. This style is scripted as (- initial attention)/ (+ sustained attention).

Identity refers to one's uniqueness and experiences as defined by social connections, emotional well-being, and intellectual capacity.

Initial attention refers to the timeliness of responses to the LIBRE prompts.

Investing in problem-solving refers to the resources and energy used to identify a problem, assess potential solutions, and reality-test workable options to determine the best course of action.

Personal values are comprised of chosen beliefs, like responsibility, loyalty, work ethic, freedom of expression, and fidelity, which are evident in the community and strongly ingrained in individuals.

Potential Engagement Style refers to guarded problem solver who approaches goal setting and problem-solving cautiously, with suspicion, hesitation, and uncertainty.

Practice in learning problem-solving involves reflecting on past actions and experiences to find solutions.

Problem-solvers are the problem actors responsible for various tasks that impact response quality, including addressing concerns, planning problem-solving phases, organizing collaboration, setting goals, managing the process, and making responsible decisions.

Problem-Solving Exchange refers to simple and complex challenges necessitating an open-minded approach to solve them.

Problem-solving requires a systematic approach to finding the best solutions for personal and professional challenges.

Relational skills refer to how well one interacts and connects with others. They comprise open and effective communication, deep listening, conveying a clear message, and engaging others.

Responsible Decision-Making is the fifth skill in socio-emotional learning and involves making positive decisions (intellectual, physical, emotional, and welfare) that benefit all involved in problem-solving.

Self refers to one's identity based on selected social community(s), intellect, physical traits, and emotional stability/skills.

Self-awareness includes accepting and appreciating our individuality, encompassing traits, qualities, emotions, behavior, and choices.

Self-management requires assuming complete responsibility for our conduct, directing our decisions and actions, and demonstrating self-control and self-regulation.

Self-reflection involves assessing the current situation and contemplating possible behavioral and action adjustments.

Problem-solver data consists of self-reported information on behavior, thoughts, values, and predispositions.

Social awareness requires connecting with others, practicing compassion, dignity, and respect.

Social context encompasses the environment and organizations that shape citizens' role in safeguarding the well-being of society.

Sustained attention includes the reactions to I-E prompts, specifically the "identify a concern" and "encourage" subsets.

LIBRE Model exchanges also referred to as problem exchanges incorporate self-reflection, collaboration, brain-storming, reality testing, planning, and action.

LIBRE Model Stick Figure Tool (LMSFT) is a problem-solving graphic organizer often used to process the LIBRE problem-solving steps.

Problem-solving exchanges involve using the SEL five competencies (self-awareness, self-management, social awareness, relationship skills, and responsible decision-making) to tackle challenges.

Venting engagement style refers to being a highly energetic procrastinator with unlimited reasons to pause and postpone action, afraid of making a wrong decision; indecisiveness contributes to problem and non-management. This style is scripted as (+) initial attention)/ (-) sustained attention).

REFERENCES

Almutairi, A. N. M. (2015). The effect of using brainstorming strategy in developing creative problem-solving skills among male students in Kuwait: A field study on Saudi Al-Karni School in Kuwait City. *Journal of Education and Practice, 6*(3), 136–145.

American Psychological Association. (2017). *Multicultural guidelines: An ecological approach to context, identity, and intersectionality.* http://www. apa.org/about/policy/muticultural-guidelines.pdf

Bandura, A. (1986). *Social foundations of thought and action.* Prentice-Hill.

Bandura, A. (1989). Social cognitive theory. In R. Vasta (Ed.), *Annals of child development* (Vol. 6, pp. 1–60). JAI Press.

Bandura, A. (1997). *Self-efficacy: The exercise of control.* Freeman.

Bandura, A. (2000). Toward a psychology of human agency. *Perspectives on Psychological Science, 1,* 164–180.

Bandura, A. (2006). Toward a psychology of human agency. *Perspectives on Psychological Science, 1*(2), 164–180.

Bronfenbrenner, U. (1979). *The ecology of human development.* Harvard University Press.

Bronfenbrenner, U. (1989). Ecological systems theory. In R. Vasta (Ed.), *Annals of child development: Six theories of child development* (Vol. 6). JAI Press.

Collaborative for Academic, Social, and Emotional Learning (CASEL). (2003). *Safe and sound: An educational leader's guide to evidence-based social and emotional learning (SEL) programs.* https://casel.org/safe-and-sound-guide-to-sel-programs/

Deckman, J. (2020). *The Aristotle model for solving complex problems.* https://jeffreydeckman.com/the-aristotle-model-for-solving-complex-problems/

Erikson, E. (1959). *Identity and the life cycle* (Psychological Issues Monograph No. 1). International Universities Press.

Erikson, E. H. (1963). *Childhood and society* (2nd ed.). Norton & Company.

Erikson, E. H. (1994). Identity and the life cycle. W.W. Norton.

Evans, R. I. (1967). *Dialogue with Erik Erickson.* Harper & Row.

Flavell, J. H. (1971). Stage-related properties of cognitive development. *Cognitive Psychology, 2,* 421–453.

Folkman, J. (2021). *8 consistent behaviors of practically perfect problem solvers.* Leadership Insights. https://www.leadershipinsights.com/8-consistent-behaviors

Freud, S. (1955). Beyond the pleasure principle. In J. Strachey (Ed. & Trans.), *The standard edition of the complete psychological works of Sigmund Freud* (Vol. 18, pp. 7–64) Hogarth Press.

Guerra, N. S. (2006). The LIBRE problem-solving model: A practical approach to problem-solving and decision-making for teachers and teacher educators. *Texas Teacher Educator's Forum, 29,* 9–14.

Guerra, N. S. (2007). LIBRE model: Engagement styles in counseling. *Journal of Employment Counseling, 44,* 2–10.

Guerra, N. S. (2009a). LIBRE stick figure tool: Graphic organizer. *Interventions in Schools and Clinics, 44*(4), 1–5.

Guerra, N. S. (2009b). Illustrations of engagement styles: Four teacher candidates. *Teacher Education & Practice, 22*(1), 95–117.

Guerra, N. S. (2015). *Clinical problem-solving case management.* Rowman & Littlefield.

Guerra, N. S. (2016). *Addressing challenges Latinos/as encounter with the LIBRE problem-solving model: Listen-identify-brainstorm-reality-test-encourage-age.* Peter Lang.

Guerra, N. S. (2022). *Teacher candidate problem-solving engagement styles: LIBRE model self-management analysis.* Information Age Publishing.

Guerra, N. S., & Carrillo-Bollinger, E. A. (2011). Engagement styles in consultation: The LIBRE model problem-solving tool. *The Dialog Journal of the Texas Educational Diagnosticians' Association, 40*(1), 4–8.

Guerra, N. S., Loera, D., Enciso, M., & Claeys, L. (2024). *Student leadership model for Hispanic-serving and emerging Hispanic-serving institutions.* Information Age Publishing.

Hadwin, A. F., Jarvela, S., & Miller, A. M. (2011). Self-regulated, coregulated, and socially shared regulation of learning. In B. J. Zimmerman, & D. H. Schunk (Eds.), *Handbook of self-regulation of learning and performance: Educational psychology handbook series.* Routledge.

Kaufman, S. B. (2020). *Transcend: The new science of self-actualization.* A Tracher Perigee Book.

Lave, J. (1993). The practice of learning. In S. Chaiklin & J. Leve (Eds.), *Understanding practice: Perspectives on activity and context* (pp. 3–32). Cambridge University Press.

Lave, J., & Wenger, E. (1991). *Situated learning: Legitimate peripheral participation*. Cambridge University Press.

Linehan, C., & McCarthy, J. (2000). Positioning in practice: Understanding participation in the social world. *Journal for the Theory of Social Behavior, 30*(4), 435–453.

Maslow, A. (1943). A theory of human motivation. *Psychological Review, 50,*370–396.

Maslow, A. (1962). *Toward a psychology of being* (3rd ed.) Wiley.

Maslow, A. (1968). *Toward a psychology of being* (2nd ed.). Van Nostrand Reinhold.

Maslow, A. (1998). *Maslow on management.* John Wiley & Sons.

Miller, P. H. (2011). *Theories of developmental psychology.* Worth Publications.

Piaget, J. (1971). The theory of stages in cognitive development. In D. B. Green, M. P. Ford, & G. B. Flanner (Eds.), *Measurement and Piaget.* McGraw-Hill.

Rogers, C. R. (1962). Toward becoming a fully functioning person. In A. W. Combs (Ed.), *Perceiving, behaving, becoming: A new focus for education.* National Education Association.

Warren, J. M. (2018). *School consultation for student success: a cognitive behavioral approach.* Springer.

Zimmerman, B. (2008). Investigating self-regulation and motivation. Historical background, methodological development, and future prospects. *American Educational Research Journal, 45*, 166–183.

ABOUT THE AUTHORS

Norma S. Guerra, PhD, is a School Psychologist, national certified school psychologist (NCSP), licensed specialist in school psychology (LSSP), and licensed professional counselor—supervisor (LPC-S). She is also Professor Emeritus at the Educational Psychology Department, College of Education and Human Development, University of Texas at San Antonio. Dr. Guerra's research is on problem-solving and human development. She has continued to research the connections between change management and personal development.

Abelardo Villarreal, PhD, is a researcher at the Academy for Teacher Excellence, University of Texas at San Antonio. Dr. Villarreal's research interests include school change, teacher and administrator professional development, school equity, and instructional materials development.

www.ingramcontent.com/pod-product-compliance
Lightning Source LLC
Chambersburg PA
CBHW070347270326
41926CB00017B/4028